10 Lessons in Localisation

Praise for this book

'In *10 Lessons in Localisation*, Dr. Sinead Walsh delivers a courageous reflection on why aid localisation so often fails to move beyond rhetoric. Drawing from her academic and lived experience, she exposes the uncomfortable truths about power, control, and accountability in the aid sector. As a scholar and practitioner of development management in Africa, I find this book a necessary and timely call for the aid sector to confront the persistent structural barriers and genuinely center the voices of communities they support.'

Prof. Dr. Rose Bakenegura Namara, Professor of Development Management, Uganda Management Institute

'Drawing on her extensive and uniquely varied practical experience in the development field, Sinead Walsh is not interested in easy platitudes about how to 'fix' international development through localisation. Recognising a complexity and a far longer history to these issues than is usually acknowledged, and drawing on detailed long term empirical research, she brings careful scrutiny and fearless analysis to the many difficult questions raised by current localisation debates around accountability, legitimacy, partnership and humility. This is a book that should be read by everyone who cares about the work NGOs do and where the NGO community is going.'

Professor David Lewis, Department of International Development at the London School of Economics and Political Science

'This book makes a powerful, timely, critical, but constructive contribution to the development effectiveness and localisation debates. Informed by lived experience and real world examples, written in an accessible and engaging tone, Sinead Walsh grapples with complex and uncomfortable questions concerning the structural, organisational and managerial barriers to localisation in the international development and humanitarian sector. The book shares insights on the evolution of mechanisms to enhance partnership, downward accountability and the more recent sector drive towards localisation. It provides a set of 10 practical recommendations for non-governmental organisations (NGOs) on how to effectively localise their operations. In light of the rapid and radical shifts within the international development and humanitarian space and collapsing institutional donor support, this book makes a timely and important contribution, offering proposals to support the transformation of NGO practices, centring the needs and interests of the communities they serve. It is a must-read for scholars, practitioners, and interested publics.'

Susan P. Murphy, Associate Professor in Sustainable Development Practice, Geography, School of Natural Sciences, Trinity College Dublin, the University of Dublin

'In *10 Lessons in Localisation*, Dr. Sinead Walsh draws on grounded experience and extensive research to offer a clear-eyed examination of the real-world challenges involved in making localisation work. In the context of shrinking development budgets, it's more important than ever to learn from past experience and confront the power dynamics and organisational behaviours that shape partnership and accountability. As someone who teaches in this field, I welcome how this book opens space for difficult but necessary conversations we need in both classrooms and organisations. A vital read for anyone serious about making localisation work.'

Tara Bedi, Assistant Professor in International Development Practice, Geography, School of Natural Sciences, Trinity College Dublin, the University of Dublin

'Based on decades of hands-on experience in the aid sector, Sinead Walsh offers sharp, instructive insights into the challenges of localisation. Drawing on robust academic evidence and vivid examples from real life, this book of hard-won lessons provides vital guidance to urgent questions facing NGOs today. Essential reading for practitioners committed to bringing about meaningful change in global development.'

Angela Crack, Professor of Civil Society, University of Portsmouth

10 Lessons in Localisation
Making aid work for communities

Dr. Sinead Walsh

Practical
ACTION
PUBLISHING

Practical Action Publishing Ltd
25 Albert Street, Rugby,
Warwickshire, CV21 2SD, UK
www.practicalactionpublishing.com

A catalogue record for this book is available from the British Library.

A catalogue record for this book has been requested from the Library of Congress.

ISBN 978-1-78853-409-3 Paperback
ISBN 978-1-78853-411-6 Electronic book

Citation: Walsh, S. (2025) *10 Lessons in Localisation: Making aid work for communities*,
Rugby, UK: Practical Action Publishing http://doi.org/10.3362/9781788534116
Since 1974, Practical Action Publishing has published and disseminated books and
information in support of international development work throughout the world.

Practical Action Publishing is a trading name of Practical Action Publishing Ltd
(Company Reg. No. 1159018), the wholly owned publishing company of Practical
Action. Practical Action Publishing trades only in support of its parent charity
objectives and any profits are covenanted back to Practical Action (Charity Reg. No.
247257, Group VAT Registration No. 880 9924 76).

Cover design by: Katarzyna Markowska, Practical Action Publishing

Typesetting by: vPrompt eServices Pvt. Ltd.

The manufacturer's authorised representative in the EU for product safety is
Lightning Source France, 1 Av. Johannes Gutenberg, 78310 Maurepas, France.
compliance@lightningsource.fr

Contents

List of Acronyms

AAIU	ActionAid International Uganda
ALPS	Accountability Learning and Planning System
LRP	Local Rights Programme
NGO	Non-governmental organisation
OD	Organisational development
PRRP	Participatory Review and Reflection Process
SPLA	Sudan People's Liberation Army
USAID	US Agency for International Development

CHAPTER ONE
Points of departure

After 20 years working and studying in the development and humanitarian sectors, in 2020 I started working on climate change. This was an area I had been keen to get into for quite a while as the impacts of climate change were becoming inescapable in the places where I had lived and worked in Africa and South Asia over the years.

While there were overlaps with the sectors I was coming from, there was also a huge amount of new stuff to get used to in the climate space, like COP negotiations and different ways of doing funding.[1] In early 2021, the Irish Government, for which I work, was asked to sign up to a set of principles for 'locally led adaptation' which were linked to a new push on localisation in the development and humanitarian sectors (World Resources Institute, 2022). One of the principles was 'Devolving decision making to the lowest appropriate level'. Another was 'Investing in local capabilities to leave an institutional legacy'. I was on familiar ground!

Partnership and capacity building

I had spent the first 10 years or so of my working life with non-governmental organisations (NGOs). I had started off working for local and international organisations in India and Rwanda. I was then in the first wave of people employed by the international NGO Concern Worldwide to work on promoting their partnerships with local NGOs, and on organising the associated capacity building on both sides to make this possible. I did this Capacity Building Advisor role in Pakistan and South Sudan. In between these stints, I did a master's thesis on the area of partnership, doing my research with Concern in India in 2004.

Working on partnership and capacity building really resonated with my values and why I had gotten into development work in the first place. Surely the momentum I saw on this in the early 2000s reflected a natural and irreversible shift to work being decided and driven more at local level.

My work on the ground taught me quickly that this was not so straightforward. I saw very different practices and potential between high-capacity partners in Gujarat, India, and very weak organisations in remote rural South Sudan, where mere survival had been the over-riding concern for decades.

After a number of years working on and researching partnership and capacity building, I developed an obsession with a related trend that became particularly prominent in the late 2000s: mechanisms to promote *downward accountability* to communities.

Downward accountability

Around this time, the international development and humanitarian NGO sectors were awash with discussions and initiatives aiming to achieve an accountability that was balanced between NGOs' upward accountability to donors, and their downward accountability to the people they intended to serve. Voluntary codes of conduct, certification initiatives, and other accountability mechanisms abounded in the sector in the late 1990s and early 2000s, and organisations were established to support and promote accountability improvement (Jordan, 2005; Lloyd et al., 2007; Omelicheva, 2004).

This concern resonated with me. My time with local and international NGOs in East Africa and South Asia had made me think that something was amiss with respect to NGOs' accountability to *intended beneficiaries*, i.e. the people we intended to provide benefits to in our projects, within the communities where development projects took place.[2]

In principle, this relationship with those we NGOs intended to serve was at the very core of our *raison d'être*. And the concept of international NGOs working in partnership with national and local NGOs, as I had been promoting, was supposed to help with strengthening this relationship with communities. But in practice, I found that so many other priorities got in the way.

I became extremely interested in the various initiatives that were setting out to fix this. My NGO, Concern, was busy making great efforts to qualify for certification for the Humanitarian Accountability Partnership (now the Core Humanitarian Standard Alliance), which was a self-regulation mechanism established in 2003 to help humanitarian NGOs orient themselves more closely to the views of their intended beneficiaries, using mechanisms like feedback sessions at community level. I started attending conferences and reading books in which NGOs discussed the best mechanisms to use to get closer to their constituents' needs.

I wanted to help NGOs get better at responding to what the communities we worked with wanted us to do. To do this, I had the idea to research what the best mechanisms for accountability to communities were, so that I could share this information across the NGO sector. A PhD seemed like a good way to go about this research. I did some homework and decided to approach NGO studies guru David Lewis at the London School of Economics (LSE) to ask him to be my PhD supervisor. He had literally written the textbook (Lewis, 2014) on NGO management, surely the perfect person to guide me on how to help fix this problem of accountability.

Our first meeting didn't go as I expected.

'You're all nice people. And intelligent', David said to me in his office in LSE, 'If NGO accountability was fixable, why haven't you figured it out by now?' I was taken aback. It was the first time anyone had suggested to me that this might not be a problem that NGOs could fix with greater effort, more knowledge, and the right mechanisms. After all, being accountable to communities was why we existed as NGOs. Right?

Over the course of the five and a half years it took me to complete my PhD while working, and with an extraordinary level of patience, David helped me to see that, as with partnership, there was a lot more going on with this issue of NGO accountability than I had originally thought, particularly underlying structural issues that didn't just go away if you had the right mechanism.

What followed, albeit slowly, was a complete transformation of how I saw the topic of NGO accountability and, more broadly, how I saw the aid sector in which I was, and remain, deeply entrenched.

The main focus of my research this time was ActionAid, the organisation which at the time seemed to have the most promising system for downward accountability, the Accountability Learning and Planning System (ALPS). I will go into a lot more detail on this later, but in short, ALPS covered a lot of what might now be termed localisation practices in areas like participation of and transparency to communities, and it included a strong partnership component.

This book

I had continued to have a working life in parallel to my studies, which continuously gave me different and useful perspectives on my research.

Soon after beginning my studies at the Social Policy Department of LSE in 2008, I left my job in Concern and the NGO sector, and began working for the Irish Government's development cooperation programme, Irish Aid.

I went straight into the NGO funding section of Irish Aid, which meant that I was still working with and on NGOs every day, albeit from more of a distance than before. This fit well with the plan for my PhD research: that I should step out of my daily work with NGOs in order to look inside in a more in-depth way and with fresh eyes.

After a few years in the NGO funding section, I spent five years in Sierra Leone from 2011 to 2016. There I worked as Ireland's Ambassador to Sierra Leone and Liberia and, for most of those years, also headed up the Irish Aid programme in the two countries.

I submitted my PhD in April 2014, but dissemination of my findings would have to wait. An Ebola outbreak started in Sierra Leone the following month.

My entire working life for about two years revolved around Ebola, whether response to or recovery from the epidemic that was (and remains) the largest Ebola epidemic in history. Irish Aid provided funding to various NGOs and worked closely with them on policy issues and humanitarian response.

Ebola brought normal life to a standstill in Sierra Leone, Liberia, and Guinea. After it was over, I left Sierra Leone and took a year off work to co-write a book with Oliver Johnson, *Getting to Zero: A Doctor and a Diplomat on the Ebola Frontline*, about the crisis (Walsh and Johnson, 2018).

I subsequently returned to Irish Aid headquarters, working on UN agencies and other multilateral organisations. After a year of this, I got the role of EU Ambassador to South Sudan, based in the capital Juba. The EU role, which included significant engagement in development and humanitarian programmes, again gave me a different vantage point from which to view NGO work.

It had always bothered me that I hadn't done enough dissemination of the findings of my PhD – which of course I thought were fascinating! But I also felt that the moment had passed in terms of the direction my career had taken. Learning about the localisation movement in the development and humanitarian sectors, and about locally led adaptation initiatives in the climate sector over the last few years changed that. I was reminded of those very same structural issues that my supervisor David had hinted at to me all those years ago and that kept arising in my work and research on downward accountability, and indeed earlier on partnership.

I was also reminded of one of my own principal learnings: that the development and humanitarian sectors are prone to what I call *trend-jumping*, whereby the latest concept or initiative is seen to be the one that will finally sort things out, but where the deeper issues are missed or ignored.

This motivated me to want to write this book, to share what I learnt on what I now saw as the earlier iterations of localisation, partnership, and downward accountability, in the hope that these might be useful for the practitioners and researchers of today.

So, what is localisation?

Localisation has become a new imperative within the humanitarian sector, and to a lesser extent the development sector, in recent years. It could also of course be called a renewed imperative since it follows on from decades of initiatives, such as those I have been involved in myself.

While there is no agreed definition of localisation, a significant section of the literature views it as a way to rethink the humanitarian and development sectors from the bottom up, highlighting the importance of greater leadership and delivery by local and national actors. The US Agency for International Development (USAID, 2022, p. 2), previously one of localisation's biggest proponents, described it as 'the set of internal reforms, actions, and behavior changes we are undertaking to ensure our work puts local actors in the lead, strengthens local systems, and is responsive to local communities'.

The term came to prominence as part of the Grand Bargain agreement in 2016 between some of the largest donors and humanitarian organisations. The main aim of the Grand Bargain is 'to improve the effectiveness and efficiency of the humanitarian action, in order to get more means into the hands of people in need' (Grand Bargain, 2025b).

The original Grand Bargain had 10 workstreams, two of which are relevant to what has become known as the localisation agenda in the intervening years. The first of these – 'More support and funding tools for local and national responders' – was particularly central, while the other focused on a 'participation revolution' aimed at involving aid recipients in the decision-making processes (Grand Bargain Secretariat, 2016).[3] The Grand Bargain energised the localisation agenda and there has been much discussion and activity in the years since.

USAID made localisation a major priority which, given its prominent position as a humanitarian donor, generated a lot of activity. However, as I write in February 2025, USAID has been shut down, although there are legal challenges pending. It is impossible to say at the moment what will happen and what implications this will have for the localisation agenda, but it is unlikely to be positive. What it probably does mean is that it will be even more important that localisation is done well, which hopefully this book will contribute to.

While the Grand Bargain focused on humanitarian actors, development actors (which are of course often the same organisations) have also taken up this localisation agenda. At the Effective Development Co-operation Summit in December 2022, 15 Development Assistance Committee (DAC) donors endorsed a statement specifically supporting locally led development (Laugharn, 2024). Numerous authors opined that the COVID-19 pandemic, by restricting monitoring opportunities by international actors, was another factor which drove this agenda forward (Barbelet et al., 2021; Robillard et al., 2021). Other authors felt that the Black Lives Matter movement brought conversations about racism and colonialism to the fore which gave localisation further prominence (Baguios et al., 2021).

How is localisation going?

After the Grand Bargain, there was a lot of focus on increasing the proportion of funding going to local and national actors with a goal of at least 25 per cent of humanitarian funding by 2020 (Grand Bargain, 2024).

In a paper in December 2021, Robillard et al. (2021, p. 20) reported that, 'Direct funding to local actors continues to be only about 3% of tracked international humanitarian funds, far short of the Grand Bargain goal of 25%'. Hugo Slim (2021, p. 2) called it 'a stunning failure'.

Academics Lina Frennesson et al. (2022, p. 2) reviewed various reports on the progress of localisation and were critical:

> the practical implementation – execution – of localization is lagging … Two vice presidents of Care Canada (2021) add: 'Despite our commitments to localization and partnership, we, like many of our peers, have been slow to change, stubbornly holding onto power and resources in the Global North and accepting donor requirements that are both archaic and inherently problematic in the name of organizational survival'. A multitude of reports reach similar conclusions: 'While there are many laudable small examples of change, a lot remains to be done. Overall progress remains slow, and there is little evidence of structural or systemic change'; 'Further progress is needed to ensure that local agencies are empowered to respond without international support'; 'Change is happening, but slowly, since fundamental blockages in the system have not been addressed'.

Another review commissioned by the Dutch Government concluded similarly stating, 'there is only limited evidence that Grand Bargain commitments on localisation drive change at the country level. Ultimately, practice has not significantly shifted to see more power and resources going to local actors' (Barbelet et al., 2021, p. 10).

Many of the issues raised in these progress summaries are unfortunately deeply familiar to me, thinking back on the partnership and downward accountability agendas over the years. Reading these very mixed reviews of the progress of localisation made me think that my experience of these agendas was worth sharing.

However, it's important to say that despite the negative aspects of such reviews and the turbulence with respect to USAID, there are still significant efforts being made on localisation and many people very committed to it. For example, there is much activity on the follow-up to the Grand Bargain, which has 68 signatories (Grand Bargain, 2023b). There is a detailed Grand Bargain Implementation

Agenda covering 2024–26 with a particular focus on localisation (Grand Bargain, 2025a). There are also monthly newsletters, compilations of good practices from signatories, National Reference Groups by country, and Caucuses by topic.

I hope that this book can contribute towards equipping practitioners and supporters of localisation in the development, humanitarian, and climate sectors to learn from experience in order to do the best possible job.

What this book is not

This book is intended to be an exploration of the challenges and the learnings on themes related to localisation from my experience and research. It's important to say that this book is not a review or judgement of the NGOs that I talk about, principally ActionAid and Concern. I researched the organisations during particular periods and in particular places on specific themes. Much time has passed and both organisations will no doubt have changed a lot since I researched or worked for them. I have not attempted to do any current research on how these themes are developing within these NGOs. I am glad to say that both organisations sent me short reflection notes having read a draft of this book and I have included these as annexes at the end of the book. I think it is also important to state my belief, based on my experience working with a large number and wide range of NGOs over the last 25 years, that the lessons and challenges that I talk about in this book are not at all unique to these two organisations.

What this book will cover

This book will discuss my experience of and research into earlier iterations of localisation, with the aim of helping those practitioners and researchers trying to make localisation work today. I will discuss 10 lessons I have learnt on partnership and downward accountability.

1. All localisation efforts, including partnership, can be difficult and need to be carefully planned according to the context.
2. Don't be constrained by political correctness: Partnership is not always the answer; communities must come first.

3. Be careful who represents the local community in partnership or other localisation initiatives, and monitor how these groups are interacting with the wider group of community members.

4. Providing strong support to localisation will have implications for the quantity and types of staff of international organisations.

5. Addressing power dynamics at community level and within NGOs themselves is central to localisation. Understanding these dynamics is a critical first step to improvements.

6. The NGO tendency for *trend-jumping* undermines the potential for localisation; NGOs need to stay the course.

7. Individual staff members' pressures and interests are highly relevant to localisation attempts and in some cases undermine them, and therefore must be recognised and understood.

8. The desire for retention of control by international organisations is real, even if it's sometimes unconscious. This should be borne in mind for localisation attempts as it may undermine them if it is not acknowledged and tackled by the organisation.

9. In a context of managerialism, NGOs are incentivised to work on what's good for perceptions; but focusing on perceptions can reduce the incentive to act for goals like localisation.

10. An NGO interested in improving its downward accountability should take a serious look at what can be done within its own governance system, where real shifts in authority can occur, as long as implementation is carefully monitored and tokenism avoided.

I will begin by providing some background to the concept of partnership, my entry point into localisation.

CHAPTER TWO
Partnership and how I came to it

Ireland, when I was growing up in the 1980s and 1990s, was a country with a high level of awareness of and activity on poverty internationally and most especially in Africa. I, or somebody I knew, was always fundraising for something or other.

In this context, deciding at the age of perhaps eight that I was going to work on poverty in Africa wasn't particularly noteworthy. Of course, I had absolutely no idea what that meant or entailed, never even visiting a developing country until I left college at the age of 22. I also didn't know anyone who had ever undertaken such an occupation, despite the plethora of Irish religious and laypeople working as nurses, teachers, and otherwise in Africa over the decades.

The little understanding I had could probably be described kindly as traditional. It came from attending talks and demonstrations and reading whatever books and pamphlets I could find in this pre-internet age. Within this worldview, international actors were squarely in leadership positions, such as the Irish non-governmental organisations (NGOs) that were dominant in our societal consciousness in those days. It was a rude but timely awakening when I moved to India to volunteer with a local human rights organisation after college and was confronted by highly self-sufficient activists who were deeply sceptical of international assistance from the West and of its motivations.

Over the course of my time volunteering with local and national NGOs in India and then working with an international NGO in Rwanda, I decided that local and national NGOs were the future. I felt that international NGOs should only be facilitating the shift to these national organisations being in control. I looked for jobs with international NGOs in this area.

I was fortunate that I was on trend in this regard. In fact, I was quite late to this particular party in the early 2000s as this shift to partnership for many organisations went back many years.

Evolution of partnership

In the period since 1945, international NGOs have gone through major changes, from being 'welfarist' and largely involved in emergency activities, to being characterised as developmental, to being associated with protest in the North and partnership with the South (Korten, 1990). While the term partnership is contested and there is certainly no agreed definition in the development sector, a simple one that I like is 'partnership between organisations involves cooperation for a specific purpose in order to achieve common objectives' (Mohiddin, 1999 cited in Brehm et al., 2004, p. 18).

The shift to partnership related to the increased strength and prominence of Southern NGOs (what we would now often call the 'Global South'). There are two broad ways to look at this shift – through a lens of solidarity or through a lens of pragmatism.

For some international NGOs, particularly from the 1970s on, 'partnership was understood as a code word to reflect humanitarian, moral, political, ideological or spiritual solidarity between NGOs in the North and South that joined together to pursue a common cause of social change' (Fowler, 2000, p. 3). Later, it was also felt that partnerships could build the capacity of southern organisations and enhance social capital by increasing trust in societies and enabling citizens to keep a space separate from the government and the market.[4]

The idealistic literature on *authentic partnership* extolled the possibilities of the increased equality, mutuality, local ownership, sustainability, and people-centred development that could arise. Using such an approach, partnership is seen as an end in itself. Some international organisations, particularly faith-based organisations, have worked in partnership since their formation, rather than focusing on direct implementation.

But changes in the external context for international NGOs, as well as, in some cases, genuine commitment to putting Southern voices to the fore, saw a huge increase in organisations 'climbing on the bandwagon' of partnership in the 1990s and thereafter (Hately, 1997). There were a lot of international organisations for which a partnership approach was a major change and the reasons for this change were a lot more functional or pragmatic.

Structural adjustment policies in the early 1980s played a role in strengthening the NGO sector in developing countries, as many civil servants laid off as a result of these policies joined the NGO sector.[5] Official donor agencies, both bilateral and multilateral, saw these Southern NGOs as a new avenue for funds. Instead of giving funds to 'ineffective' Southern governments or to, often costly, international NGOs, they started to donate funds directly to Southern NGOs (Malhotra, 1997).

These developments then begged the question: what is the value of international NGOs? If it can be seen as more efficient and/or effective to fund Southern NGOs directly, why do any donors need international NGOs to stand in the middle and add to costs? Surely Southern NGOs have a more legitimate connection to the poor and have a superior knowledge of possible solutions to poverty? Why then involve outsiders? These were the questions that led to what Malhotra (1997, p. 18) termed the 'institutional survival concerns' of international NGOs.

These concerns intensified when governments, such as those in the UK, the US, and Canada, started sharply decreasing their aid budgets after 1990. Increased numbers of international NGOs also led to fundraising in their home countries becoming more competitive. Thus, international NGOs faced a double funding crunch, whose basic root was their questionable legitimacy to work in Southern countries when Southern organisations could do so (Malhotra, 1997).

Partly due to these institutional survival concerns, and partly due to genuine conviction, many international NGOs redefined their role, to seek their value-added in the development process and to prove it to donors. One way in which they did this was in moving away from direct implementation and forming partnerships, often involving capacity building of local partners to avoid being *just a donor*.

Concern Worldwide

Concern Worldwide was undertaking precisely this kind of shift when I saw their job advertisement in 2002. An Irish-based international NGO, Concern had a strong history of direct implementation and had decided to do more work in partnership.

The organisation was founded in Dublin in 1968 in response to the civil war in Nigeria and the ensuing famine in Biafra. It began as an emergency relief organisation, responding, for example, to the crisis which accompanied the creation of the state of Bangladesh in 1971. Over the years, Concern became increasingly involved in long-term development programmes as well as emergencies, and in the late 1990s took its first steps towards partnership.

Its 1998 Strategic Plan contained a commitment that each country programme should 'provide ongoing support towards the development of a minimum of one local organisation' during the five year period of the plan (Concern Worldwide, 1998, p. 15). The second strategic plan of 2002, just when I joined the organisation, went much further by having as an indicator that, 'by the end of the plan almost all non-emergency projects and a substantial proportion of emergency projects will be operated with or through local partners' (Concern Worldwide, 2002, p. 17).

In 2002, while I was working for another international NGO (Population Services International) on health and HIV/AIDS in the south of Rwanda, I was attracted to Concern's job advertisement for Capacity Building Advisors to push forward this agenda. I did this role for Concern in Pakistan and in South Sudan over the following five years. The next chapter begins with a case study from my time in South Sudan.

CHAPTER THREE
Context, context, context

When I was working in pre-independence South Sudan in the mid-2000s with Concern, one of my jobs was supporting a local NGO working on HIV awareness at community level. Given high HIV rates in neighbouring countries such as Uganda and Kenya, and high rates of polygamy, we were concerned that South Sudanese people might be at high risk and so we had recently taken on this partner.

One day, sitting in our office *tukul* (hut), I came across a discrepancy in this partner's finances. It wasn't particularly sophisticated, so it was quite easy to spot. Our finance team cross-checked it and agreed with the diagnosis. It was a small amount of money, but it was clearly indicative of dodgy dealings.

After further investigation, the nature of the fraud seemed to be that some of the money given to the local NGO and budgeted for activities on the ground, was being routed instead to the NGO leadership, who were based in Nairobi in Kenya, for their personal use. Having a leadership based in Nairobi was not uncommon in those days given the remoteness of where we were working.

What to do about this was another question and this was not at all straightforward.

To my colleagues and I, the desired outcome of this situation was clear: end the relationship with the partner's leadership, get the assets back that had been purchased with Concern's money (motorbikes and laptops), but try to find a way to still work with the local field staff of the NGO, who were based in our local area, if at all possible. We felt that the field staff were sincere and were doing a good job on building critical community awareness on HIV. However, getting to that outcome, in that context, was going to be incredibly complicated and possibly dangerous.

The region of South Sudan at that time was fragile and quite unstable, despite a recent peace agreement having been signed between the rebel forces – the Sudan People's Liberation Army (SPLA) – and the Sudanese Government in Khartoum. We were based in a remote area with no electricity, no phone lines, no running water, and certainly no police. The SPLA were de facto in charge and had an administration set up in a town called Rumbek, which at that time was a day or more away from where we were by car, depending greatly on the weather and the car.

In general, I was concerned about the response of the leadership of the partner organisation in Nairobi who I expected would react very badly to losing their livelihood. Complicating things further, the leaders of the organisation were linked to the SPLA, and one was an ex-combatant who had been seriously injured in the war. I knew that we needed SPLA support to end the partnership, as you needed their support for pretty much anything you wanted to do. But it was hard for me to imagine the SPLA leadership either locally or in Rumbek taking Concern's side against their own people, let alone taking our side against ex-combatants.

But what choice did we have? The amount that had been misappropriated was small, but there was still no way Concern was going to accept this fraud or continue to work with this leadership.

I called my boss in Nairobi and outlined a plan. I stressed that this plan was very risky. While I didn't think anything serious would actually happen and while we had ideas to reduce the risk, I told her that we should anticipate the possibility of death threats if we went ahead. It wouldn't be the first time Concern had seen such threats in the region in recent months. She was totally supportive and agreed we should take the risk, because it was the right thing to do. We proceeded nervously.

The first step in the plan was to get the local partner's other funder on board. This was a faith-based international organisation that, as a matter of principle and policy, gave a lot of autonomy to their local partners, so I was a bit concerned that it would be hard to get them on board with what they might see as a tough approach. They visited South Sudan from their base in Nairobi only occasionally, and so didn't have the day-to-day local engagement with partners that we had in Concern. However, their programme officer, when I spoke with her, was pragmatic and clued in and she immediately pledged their support. We worked together to commission an independent audit so that we would have external evidence to back up our findings.

The next step was political support. I went to Rumbek to meet the relevant SPLA director, who was responsible for all NGO activity in South Sudan. He had a good reputation, but I was still concerned given the circumstances. To my relief, it went very well. Rather than instinctively siding with his former SPLA colleagues, he expressed anger that money provided for South Sudan was ending up in Nairobi – it was clear that this was far from being the first time he had come across this kind of issue. He pledged his full support to our planned actions.

With this backing, we secured the support of local SPLA leadership, and with their help we successfully seized the organisation's assets early one morning. We subsequently helped the field staff of the organisation to establish themselves as a new organisation and we were able to continue the HIV awareness work with them, albeit with a lot more supervision and support given that they were a brand-new organisation.

So what did I learn from this experience?

I learnt (and this will underlie all the lessons in this book) that partnership between international and local organisations – one important aspect of what is now often referred to as localisation – can be hard. It can be extremely hard and we shouldn't underestimate this. And, more specifically, I learnt that much depends on the context.

Lesson 1: All localisation efforts, including partnership, can be difficult and need to be carefully planned according to the context.

My prior work on partnership had taken place in very different contexts, which reinforced this lesson. Before I got to South Sudan in 2005, I had been working with Concern on partnership and capacity building in Pakistan and India, having also worked in India previously myself for local and national organisations.

In Pakistan, from the office in Quetta, in the remote and very poor province of Balochistan, Concern had been working with Afghan refugees near the border on basic needs, as well as with the host population. The refugee crisis we were working on followed the US-led bombing campaign in 2001. Our programmes were around food security, water and sanitation, and basic livelihoods. My role was to support existing local NGO partners and Concern staff to build their capacities, as well as to identify new local partners.

The context in Balochistan and over the border in Afghanistan was quite unstable and our experience working with partners was quite mixed as a result, with one partner in particular being quite engaged in trying to ameliorate conflict dynamics, which, while positive, made it more complicated for us to both try to support them and hold them to account for their activities.

After my time in Pakistan, I began a master's degree in Development Studies at University College Dublin. As part of this, I travelled to India with Concern in 2004 to research a thesis on partnership. As had been the case in Pakistan, Concern's main office in the country at that time was not in the capital city of Delhi, but in the eastern state of Orissa, which was one of the poorest states in India at that time. This was therefore the base of my research. Concern had responded to the 2001 earthquake in the western state of Gujarat and had some local partners there, so I also travelled to Gujarat to interview partners. All in all, for my research, I conducted 65 interviews, a questionnaire, and a workshop, working with local partners, Concern staff, other donor organisations, and other stakeholders in Orissa, Gujarat, Delhi, and Bangalore.[6]

Some of the organisations and individuals I worked with or researched in India were some of the strongest organisations and wisest individuals I have come across in my career (to this day). While it wasn't always smooth sailing, with shortcomings on our side in Concern as well as with partners, the partners were generally strong and the partnerships worked fairly well.

At the other side of the spectrum, in fact at the extreme other end of the spectrum, South Sudan was just starting to emerge from a very long war at the time I went there in January 2005, and it was one of the poorest regions in the world. Because of the peace process, the Comprehensive Peace Agreement having been signed the week after I began the job, South Sudan was largely considered to be a post-emergency or *transition* setting. Concern hired me because the organisation was trying to transition from emergency relief to development work. I found that there was something important about these kinds of transition settings when it came to partnership.

Transition settings

Within the development and humanitarian sectors over the years, I have found that there is a large degree of acceptance that in emergency situations there are serious challenges to international NGOs working in partnership. But there is less consideration of transition settings. The problem with talking about transition settings is that many places don't seem to actually move from emergency to development. This is why we increasingly talk these days about countries in chronic crises, which is a far better way, unfortunately, to describe a country like South Sudan or parts of Pakistan.

I have spent a lot of time working in these settings and have observed that international donors, including NGOs, tend to arrive in large numbers with huge budgets to be spent quickly. Often donors, particularly NGO donors, have mandates which require, or at least strongly prefer, that they spend these budgets through national or local NGOs, since the country is no longer in a full-blown emergency.

Of course, almost by definition, these areas emerging from conflict or other disasters often have fragile social, political, and economic environments and are unlikely to have strong or developed NGOs which can absorb these large amounts of funding in a way that provides significant benefit to poor and marginalised people.

There can thus be a strong incentive for entrepreneurs to establish NGOs more for their own livelihoods than for the good of the wider community. As I experienced, corruption and abuse of NGO status are unfortunately not uncommon occurrences in the NGO sector and the mushrooming of organisations due to the easy availability of funds accentuates this problem (Clark, 1991; Fowler, 1997, 2005; Holloway, 1998).

However, rather than capturing these basic facts of low capacity and the risk of insincere organisations in their context analysis and adjusting accordingly, donors and NGOs often continue to try to work through local NGOs in transition contexts in a similar way that they would in more stable development contexts. In my experience, the effects of this are often negative and problematic.

International donors and NGOs interested in localisation therefore have a significant role to play by disaggregating their approaches to localisation, partnership, and indeed capacity building depending on the context and the individual partner.

So, for example, in Concern we needed to be much more hands-on in South Sudan. In retrospect, in the case study I talk about above, we should have had a stronger partner selection process at the outset to try to weed out the issues we ended up experiencing.[7] On the positive side, we did have close monitoring of and engagement with our partners, including capacity building, which was appropriate, and that close engagement meant that we were able to quickly detect the problem that emerged. In fact, my job had been created by Concern precisely for this strong engagement.

This lesson on context for me is intricately linked to a second, possibly more controversial lesson that I will discuss in the next chapter – that partnership is not always the answer.

CHAPTER FOUR
Partnership is not always the answer

I had read a lot of partnership literature in the years I worked with Concern on the topic, to try to get guidance for my work, some of which I discussed earlier. Much of the literature spoke very positively about the potential of partnerships for sustainable and locally driven development, and encouraged international NGOs to hand over control and decision-making powers to their local partners.

The literature was skewed towards idealism. This very much fit with my values, but at the same time, I discovered that it was not all that helpful in terms of providing guidance for work on the ground where I found a wide variety of contexts and hence possibilities for partnership, as the case study from South Sudan demonstrates. While few people argue with the premise that development processes and, as far as possible, humanitarian emergencies, need to be locally owned and managed, much of what was being written or said publicly about partnership when I was working on it was more about what should be, rather than what actually was. This was not very helpful when the reality on the ground was difficult and messy, as it usually was.

At worst, I found that taking an overly idealistic approach to partnership could be actively harmful to the objectives that Concern and other NGOs were trying to achieve.

This last point is critical. My approach, or what evolved to be my approach over the years, was that partnership is not an end in itself. While working through national and local actors was my preference, I wasn't prepared to sacrifice why I was working in development in the first place, which was to try to provide assistance to people living in poverty.

To be clear, I doubt there is anyone out there who says that they are prepared to sacrifice development outcomes for partnership, but some of the literature out there and indeed some international NGO policies and international NGO staff I have met over the years would seem to lean in that direction.

I experienced this in relation to the fraud situation in South Sudan. As I mentioned, the other international faith-based NGO which provided funding to the local NGO was based in Nairobi and made only occasional visits to monitor their funding. There were quite a few organisations which worked in this manner in South Sudan in those days and I personally felt that this was problematic in that context. To be clear, in the case of many organisations that I knew, it was not simply a decision on their part related to practicalities or costs, i.e. having only a limited number of offices for these reasons. It was also very much an ideological choice, to give their partners adequate space and autonomy. Again, I am all for that in principle and, in many contexts, it is entirely appropriate. But I would venture, it was rarely appropriate in South Sudan in 2005. From my experience there with various organisations, supporting local partners from a distance was not the best way to support communities.

I was glad to learn later that the international faith-based NGO in question came to a similar conclusion and changed their system in the subsequent years (not just in South Sudan but more broadly) to have more field offices to be based closer to their partners on an ongoing basis, particularly in difficult contexts.

I believe that the principle of solidarity partnership from a distance was genuine for the international NGO in this case. But, in my experience, it is very easy for political correctness on these kinds of issues to creep in, become dominant and steer thinking as to what is acceptable or not. We need to be careful that political correctness doesn't dictate what the right thing to do is in terms of outcomes for the intended beneficiaries of our work.

The risk of political correctness

I encountered this issue of political correctness in South Sudan. I was involved in creating a network of international NGOs interested in collaborating on how we could work better in partnership with South Sudanese NGOs. This was a popular concept at the time given the post-emergency transition I mentioned above, and we grew quickly to about 60 international NGO members. However, even though I was chairing the network in its first year, I found that I was somewhat of an outlier in the Steering Committee in terms of my views.

For example, I wanted to give a presentation to a meeting of the network about the case study I described above of the fraud. I thought it was really important that we based the network on real-life examples rather than theory or rhetoric. I called the presentation 'When Partnership Goes Wrong'. But I got a lot of pushback from other international NGOs who were concerned that this would be overly negative and might turn newly arrived international NGOs off partnership, and perhaps even come across as unfairly stereotyping South Sudanese people.

I was very confused by this. The case study was factual, and fraud was unfortunately not uncommon in the context at the time. What good would we be as a network if we only focused on positives in the context or, worse still, on the theory of how we would like things to be? I managed to negotiate still giving the presentation, with some caveats in the beginning that, of course, this did not represent all South Sudanese NGOs. In the end, the presentation was well received particularly by more operational organisations that had a local field presence.

This has mostly been my experience over the years: the closer the people I am talking to are to ground realities, the more they welcome frank discussions on the problems with partnership or other aspects of localisation. Whereas I often get pushback from colleagues who are working more from a distance and who are perhaps closer to principles than to practice.

Lest that sound condescending, I do think there can be an advantage at times to being further from the action and closer to the principles. International NGO staff members, by definition, have a vested interest in the status quo being retained, with secure and relatively well-paid jobs, some of which could and should be at risk if a meaningful shift to partnership happens with more of the direct implementation being done by national or local partners. This might not motivate individual staff members, but it is a consideration. So, challenges from colleagues further away from the action are important, as change often doesn't come from those who benefit from the current system.

But I still maintain that we need to avoid being swayed by politically correct rhetoric, including in the area of partnership.

I have come to believe that partnership is not always the best answer for the communities involved if local or national partners with capacity and sincerity are not available. This, however, is often controversial.

There is an argument that some people have made to me over the years that there are always potential local partners out there and that international organisations have a responsibility to find and nurture them in every context. But I'm not convinced. I have worked in remote areas where we could find no local organisations at all, or at least none with interest or capacity to do development or humanitarian work. Granted one can often work with some individuals to establish an organisation. International organisations have frequently created local organisations in these circumstances, but I would be very wary of this, having seen too many examples in different countries, where organisations established as vehicles to receive donor funding have gone awry.

My experiences of partnership in South Sudan, Pakistan, and India (and later in Uganda, Sierra Leone, and Liberia) were all different of course. I have worked with national or local partners who achieved far more impact than the international NGO could have without them. But just as I concluded that context should be a major consideration, I also conclude that partnership is not always the right way forward if you are primarily concerned, as I am, with impact for communities.

Lesson 2: Don't be constrained by political correctness: Partnership is not always the answer. Communities must come first.

I would argue that there are a lot of ways to promote localisation, and partnership with local NGOs is just one mechanism, albeit an important one. Moving to partnership with the same speed and scale in post-emergency areas like South Sudan, or a number of other countries in Africa or elsewhere with extremely nascent civil societies, or even moving to partnership universally within large countries like India or Kenya, which are seen to have generally well-developed civil societies, can be counter-productive and, indeed, can prevent benefits reaching the intended target group: poor and marginalised people.

At the same time, we shouldn't jump to a negative conclusion. Back to my first lesson: we should do a thorough context analysis (preferably, actually, get external actors to do it) before we conclude that there are no viable partnership options out there, guarding against our own vested interests and status quo bias. If we do conclude that it's not the time for partnership, we should then ask ourselves, how can we promote localisation in this situation? For example, later in this book, I will be looking at how localisation can be promoted through the concept of downward accountability.

Before that, in the next few chapters, I will introduce my research with ActionAid on accountability and after that, look at some of their experiences with partnership.

CHAPTER FIVE
The problems with NGO accountability

After returning from South Sudan, I worked for Concern in their Dublin headquarters, supporting country programmes to work more on advocacy and human rights. At the same time, I became extremely interested in work some colleagues of mine were doing on downward accountability. In particular, Concern was trying to get certification from a new initiative called the Humanitarian Accountability Partnership which meant that we had to get very systematic about how we were getting feedback from the communities we worked with and ensuring that we used this feedback to inform our decisions.

This accountability work appealed to me in the same way as partnership had, as a way to try to close the gap between what our intended beneficiaries wanted and what we were actually doing. Around that time, I started my PhD research at the London School of Economics (LSE) in order to try to understand better what initiatives might work best to help NGOs achieve this goal.

When I began this research, I discovered a couple of basic things in the first few months with helpful prods from my PhD supervisor. The first was that I had never really defined what I meant by accountability and, it turned out, it was pretty complicated.

Definition of accountability

After doing some homework on this, one simple and widely accepted definition of accountability in the literature stood out, that of academic Richard Mulgan, who produced a series of writings reviewing the concept of accountability across public and private sectors. Mulgan (2000, p. 555) spoke of the 'core sense' of accountability as 'being called "to account" to some authority for one's actions'. He inferred three main features of accountability from this definition:

> it is *external*, in that the account is given to some other person or body outside the person or body being held accountable; it involves *social interaction and exchange*, in that one side, that calling for the account, seeks answers and rectification while the other side, that being held accountable, responds and accepts sanctions; it implies *rights of authority*, in that those calling for an account are asserting rights of superior authority over those who are accountable, including the rights to demand answers and to impose sanctions. (emphasis in original)

This seemed fairly straightforward and uncontroversial as a definition, until I realised that this was often not how we were using the term in the NGO sector. This was due, in particular, to the hierarchical authority relationship within which an actor or entity is held to account in Mulgan's definition. When we think of examples, like politicians being accountable to voters, it's clear that citizens have the authority of the vote to wield. Similarly, customers pay for goods and services which gives them authority if something goes wrong.

However, most NGO practitioners writing in the literature at that time defined accountability in a way that allowed for intended beneficiaries to hold NGOs to account on the basis of *moral authority*. This authority had to be moral because NGOs have not been voted on by the populations they intended to serve, nor have they been paid by them.

For instance, the Humanitarian Accountability Partnership (2013), which aimed to make 'humanitarian action accountable to beneficiaries', defined accountability as the 'responsible use of power'. A similar definition was used in a paper written by David Bonbright of Keystone – a UK organisation which helps organisations improve their social performance by harnessing feedback – along with an academic, Srilatha Batliwala. The authors noted that 'accountability is the way those affected by power can hold power to account' (Bonbright and Batliwala, 2007, p. 4).

In other words, NGO authors were redefining accountability to be more in line with their values. With my own NGO hat on, this made perfect sense to me. After all, I was starting this research because I believed that NGOs should be downwardly accountable – that they should be more responsive to and transparent with community members.

But trying to take a step back from my preferences and my particular values, I had to acknowledge that it was problematic that the issue of 'authority' seemed to be being fudged here in the NGO definitions. I had seen enough power dynamics in my work to know that there was a consequence to the fact that NGOs were neither voted in nor paid for by their intended beneficiaries. But they were, of course, paid by their donors. Thus, my concern was that changing the definition of accountability to suit our ideals could serve to camouflage issues around power and authority but, crucially, would not make them go away. I will come back later in this book to the key issue of power and how it affects NGO attempts to be downwardly accountable.

History of NGO accountability

The second thing I discovered in the early period of my research was that the imbalance in NGO accountability had a much longer history than I had realised. The initiatives on accountability in the development NGO sector at this time, the late 2000s, were generally quite new, having been established since the early 2000s. This had initially suggested to me that accountability was a fairly new concern for the sector. However, when I read further, I discovered that this was far from the case.

Rather, the first significant references to NGO accountability in the literature emerged all the way back in 1987 when the *World Development* journal published a special issue on NGOs. The interest of the journal's managing editor in having this focus was catalysed by the 'rapidly increasing involvement' of NGOs in development assistance due, in part, to the recent 'ideological' trend of significant governmental funding of NGOs that I discussed earlier (Drabek, 1987, p. vii). Similarly, Edwards and Hulme's (1996) widely cited edited volume on NGO accountability was motivated by the scenario in which donors were increasingly contracting NGOs to provide welfare services. Both of these early publications expressed serious concerns about what they viewed as an imbalance of accountability with respect to NGOs, whereby intended beneficiaries often got left behind when accountability to donors was prioritised. This issue had persisted as the dominant theme in the development literature on NGO accountability.

Furthermore, I was struck by the fact that, as my PhD supervisor had alluded to in our first conversation, there was more going on in this area than I had realised. Apart from the issue being identified, numerous discussions had taken place and numerous attempts had been initiated to resolve this accountability imbalance problem over the years.

There was a 'staggering growth' in NGO accountability and development effectiveness initiatives from the mid-1990s to the 2010s (ActionAid, 2010b, p. 3). Initiatives such as voluntary codes of conduct, certification initiatives, and other accountability mechanisms had abounded, and organisations such as the Humanitarian Accountability Partnership, One World Trust, International NGO Accountability Network, Keystone Accountability, Sphere Standards, and Compas Qualité had been established to promote accountability improvement at a global level (Omelicheva, 2004; Jordan, 2005; Keystone and AccountAbility, 2006; Lloyd et al., 2007; Zarnegar Deloffre, 2010). In addition, there had been numerous codes of conduct and self-regulation mechanisms established at a national level, such as in the 22 African countries captured in Gugerty's (2010) survey on self-regulatory initiatives on the continent.

When I did a thorough review of the literature on NGO accountability, I found 40 articles that identified NGO accountability as problematic and outlined ideas for how NGOs could improve their accountability, often with specific initiatives being described.[8] This initially seemed very positive. However, a key weakness of the literature was that there was often no evidence that these ideas had actually changed practice within an NGO context, or even that they had been tried at operational level. For instance, Brown and Jagadananda (2007) describe the code of conduct of Ethiopian NGOs, the Organizational Self-Analysis tool for NGOs in India, and the Keystone initiative among others, but do not give any indication of how these are operating in practice.

Surprisingly, given the abundance of ideas and initiatives in the literature aimed at balancing NGOs' accountability between donors and intended beneficiaries, I could only find twelve articles that looked at NGOs' actual practice, and seven of these were about the same initiative, ActionAid's Accountability Learning and Planning System (ALPS) initiative, which I will describe below.

The obvious question was why this issue was rearing its head for this number of years, decades in fact, without apparent improvements in practice? Oddly though, it did not appear that this question was being asked by NGOs and others in the development sector; the focus was more on launching new initiatives.

As I read more, I concluded that the tendency to focus on how to achieve balanced accountability in practical terms, had militated against improving understanding of why imbalances in accountability exist, and whether there were fundamental, structural blockages that were hindering improvements to downward accountability.

Rather, the mood in much of the development literature was optimistic and suggested that NGOs simply needed to try harder to put policies and principles of downward accountability into practice. I confess that this is precisely what I had thought myself before I had started to read up on the topic! But then ironically, despite an apparent bias towards practice on the ground, there was very little in the NGO literature describing actual attempts of NGOs trying to improve the balance of their accountabilities at the operational level.

I used these gaps in the NGO accountability literature as the starting point for my own field research. I wanted to study actual attempts of NGOs to put their downward accountability principles into practice, but I also wanted to do this with an openness to consider structural barriers that might exist, given that the problem was so long-standing. Harking back to my first meeting with my supervisor David, I wanted to understand before I presumed to make recommendations. The questions were who, what, and where to research to get these insights.

These questions were not, in fact, difficult to answer. When I reviewed the literature on what development NGOs had been doing in this space, one NGO, ActionAid, stood out, far ahead of the rest of the pack. In the next chapter, I introduce ActionAid's accountability journey.

CHAPTER SIX
Enter ActionAid

ActionAid International was founded in 1972 in the UK as a child sponsorship agency, originally named Action in Distress (Ebrahim and Gordon, 2011). Their latest organisational strategy summary is similar to when I was doing my research, the aim being:

> to build international momentum for social, economic and environmental justice, driven by people living in poverty and exclusion. In practice, this means working closely with people living in poverty and exclusion, civil society organisations, social movements and supporters. Together, we deliver grass-roots programmes, provide emergency relief and campaign for things such as women's economic rights, tax justice and climate justice. (ActionAid, 2024c)

ActionAid operates as a federation of 46 country-level organisations worldwide and its expenditure in 2023 was €255 million (ActionAid, 2024a). These 46 countries are either net fund-raising countries (mostly in the North) or net fund-spending countries (mostly in the South) where most programming takes place. ActionAid has been headquartered in Johannesburg since 2004. I selected ActionAid for my research because of an innovative system they had created in 2000 called the Accountability Learning and Planning System (ALPS).

Why was ALPS created?

As discussed above, the 1990s saw changing roles for international development NGOs from the Global North. Southern NGOs became increasingly prominent and thus Northern international NGOs engaged more and more in partnership and capacity building with their Southern counterparts. ActionAid was no different, but attempted a more radical transformation than most of its counterparts.

Up until the late 1990s, ActionAid was a community development organisation, working largely in a service delivery mode in a wide range of sectors such as health, education, and income generation. Its funds were raised largely from members of the public in the UK, who sponsored children within the communities in which ActionAid worked, i.e. they contributed a monthly amount in a particular child's name. The funding modality of child sponsorship had implications for how ActionAid worked, as the organisation focused on certain geographical areas for approximately 10 years, in order to work with the same groups of children and fulfil the promises made to the sponsors, such as that the child would finish school. At the time of my research, these kinds of local programme units in ActionAid were referred to as Local Rights Programmes (LRPs).

A new Chief Executive, Salil Shetty, took up the role in 1998. Salil, an Indian national, was one of a new cadre of Southern leaders in ActionAid, and working with the other leaders and a group of Northern staff and board members interested in change, he launched an ambitious new strategy for ActionAid, *Fighting Poverty Together*, which took effect in 1999. The strategy focused on how the organisation worked, more so than on what it did.

The strategy's main focus was to tackle the root causes of poverty through adopting a *human rights-based approach* to development (ActionAid, 1999). This involved moving away from ActionAid's traditional approach of mainly delivering services to needy people, towards empowering citizens to seek accountability from their governments. The language within ActionAid documentation changed from speaking about 'beneficiaries' to speaking about 'rights-holders'. This new direction had enormous implications for how ActionAid worked as an organisation and for its accountabilities.

The first implication related to partnership. The strategy called for ActionAid to work with significantly more partners at local and national levels. The partnership approach was an attempt to move ActionAid programming closer to rights-holders, with local groups of community members empowered to make decisions on how best to improve their lives and livelihoods. In many countries, particularly in

Africa, partnership was a radical change from the past, as ActionAid had previously tended to directly implement programmes.

Second, the *Fighting Poverty Together* strategy called for a major change in ActionAid's governance system (ActionAid, 1999). Up to that time, ActionAid had been governed by a board in the UK. A key element of the new strategy was 'internationalisation', whereby power and authority were to be decentralised, ultimately to rights-holders at community level. Internationalisation, as it evolved during the strategy period, meant that ActionAid countries – including Northern fundraising offices such as the UK and Southern country programmes – would become self-governing, semi-autonomous entities within the global ActionAid network, with their own country-level general assemblies and boards. These country-level structures would then send representatives to a global general assembly and board, which would govern the entire organisation. Furthermore, ActionAid would move its headquarters from the UK to the Global South (ultimately South Africa).

In order to test the organisation's readiness to undertake the journey called for by the *Fighting Poverty Together* strategy, Salil Shetty commissioned a group of consultants to undertake an organisational review called *Taking Stock* (Dichter, 1999).[9] The review was 'excoriating' and 'devastating' (Scott-Villiers, 2002, p. 431). It categorically stated that ActionAid was not ready to implement the planned strategy. It painted a picture of a heavily bureaucratic, non-transparent, sometimes arrogant organisation which was working mainly at the local level on symptoms of poverty, rather than on deeper structural issues. The review concluded that the organisation was generally not learning or reflecting, not innovative or outward looking, and not accountable to the poor.

The *Taking Stock* review was a shock to many in ActionAid and catalysed significant energy around reform of the organisation to enable the implementation of the *Fighting Poverty Together* strategy. Various processes and initiatives began, some of them painful and leading to termination of long-standing staff, as the organisation shifted to partnership (Newman, 2011). At the country programme level, some country directors carried out reform processes, notably the new Indian country directors in Uganda and Kenya (Helman and Moore, 2002; Wallace and Kaplan, 2003). It was in this context of energised reform that the next major shift occurred: the creation of ALPS (David and Mancini, 2004).

Beginnings of ALPS

The *Taking Stock* review was particularly critical of ActionAid's system of planning, monitoring, and reporting, which it found to be extremely time-consuming, while bearing little fruit in terms of bringing the voices of poor people into the organisation's decision-making (Dichter, 1999). As Salil Shetty noted:

> A growing concern voiced by staff and local partners in recent years has been the disproportionate amount of time and effort that is going into meeting ActionAid's planning and reporting requirements. If it were only a question of wrong priorities, the problem could easily be rectified by reordering time allocation. The bigger risk is the spread of a culture of bureaucratisation and disempowerment of staff, partners and ultimately the poor people that we work with. (ActionAid, 2000, p. 1)

This was not a new criticism. ActionAid had been struggling internally for several years with its Annual Planning and Reporting System, which emphasised standardised and linear planning and upward reporting for donors, and which was viewed as bureaucratic and cumbersome (Scott-Villiers, 2002). For instance, annual reports of country programmes could take several months to prepare. Various efforts had been made to try to reform the Annual Planning and Reporting System and had failed. The *Taking Stock* review provided the impetus for a new process to reform these systems.

A committee was established to create a new system, including senior programme staff and Robert Chambers, a member of the UK board of trustees and a leader in participatory methodologies for development (David and Mancini, 2011). In 2000, this work led to the birth of ALPS.

Salil Shetty, in his introduction to ALPS, set out the aims for the system. ALPS was expected to help operationalise the *Fighting Poverty Together* strategy by:

> fostering a culture where staff and partners do not have the comfort of relying on rules and procedures but have to use their own initiative to achieve our common mission; significantly improving the quality and quantity of interaction

with poor people and other partners; raising the premium on reflection, analysis and learning that can be converted into improved programme and advocacy actions; ensuring that decisions are taken as close to the point where their consequences are felt and bringing the concerns and aspirations of poor people into the centre of our decision making. (ActionAid, 2000, p. ii)

What is ALPS?

ALPS is a system outlining the planning, review, and reporting requirements of the organisation, among other elements. What was remarkable about ALPS when it was launched was its demonstration of ActionAid's efforts to align its programming systems with its values, particularly around the prioritisation of downward accountability. Importantly, ALPS is not limited to processes and requirements, but also details the attitudes and behaviours of staff that would be necessary to promote accountability, learning, and planning within these processes. Figure 6.1 outlines the components of the system.

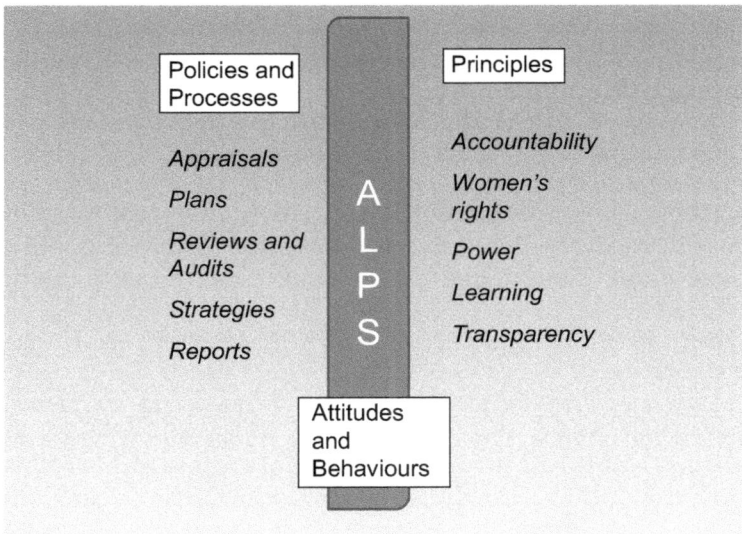

Figure 6.1 Components of ALPS
Source: Author's own

External reviews of ALPS

When I started my research, ALPS was, hands down, the best-known accountability initiative in the development sector. The system had been promoted by ActionAid, and was perceived by other authors as being at the cutting edge of NGO accountability practice (Guijt, 2007; Jordan, 2007). External authors tended to particularly applaud ActionAid for its downward accountability system, which encouraged learning, such as Brown (2008) in an article on accountability within transnational civil society. Ebrahim and Gordon (2011) also discussed ALPS favourably in a paper focused on ActionAid's governance processes.

ActionAid often featured in the NGO literature as the only positive example of an organisation practising balanced accountability that authors named. For instance, ActionAid was cited positively in an article by Koch (2008), which argued that NGOs should be held as accountable as governmental donors within the aid effectiveness agenda. In a review of publications on learning and social change, Guijt (2007, p. 34) stated that '[ALPS] is arguably the most discussed and quoted shift by an international NGO to ensure that its Strategic priorities and principles are reflected in its procedures for learning and accountability'. From my review of this literature, this was not arguable; no other organisational example even came close to being cited as much as ALPS.

However, it should not be assumed that these authors had knowledge of ALPS at implementation level. One World Trust, a London-based think-tank on accountability, rated ActionAid the highest of all 11 international NGOs reviewed in its 2006 rankings on accountability (Blagescu and Lloyd, 2006). However, when I looked into the fine print, I discovered that this ranking was based on ActionAid's policies, such as ALPS and the organisation's 'Open Information Policy', rather than its practices, which were not reviewed.

Similar to One World Trust, very few of the authors mentioned above were basing their assessment of ALPS on any study of practice. Neither did they claim to. Most of the references to ALPS were very brief and usually, at most, cited ActionAid publications as references, rather than any independent study. In fact, most authors appeared to be basing their positive assessment simply on the existence of the ALPS document.

Having concluded that there was no substantial external study of ALPS, I then turned to the internal literature by ActionAid staff themselves to seek out studies of practice on the ground.

Internal reviews of ALPS

In the early years of ALPS, while practitioners within ActionAid were considering what the system meant for them, some staff members were already presenting on ALPS in external literature and at conferences. In particular, seven articles on ALPS were written using data collected up to 2004 (although some were published later) and six of these were written by ActionAid staff members, along with regular consultants linked to the organisation (Chapman et al., 2003; David and Mancini, 2003, 2004, 2011; David et al., 2006; Okwaare and Chapman, 2006).

This literature on ALPS comprised a significant contribution to the sparse empirical literature on NGO accountability that I discussed earlier. Films on ALPS were also made by the Kenya country programme in 2007 and the Bangladesh country programme in 2008. Presentations were given by ActionAid staff members at various external conferences, some of which I attended. In one of their articles, David and Mancini (2004), former staff members who were central to the implementation of ALPS, spoke of the frequent requests to give talks on ALPS from its early days.

The articles, films, and presentations on ALPS followed a fairly consistent pattern: they reflected on why there was a need for a re-balancing of accountabilities, described how ActionAid created ALPS in an attempt to do this, and outlined ALPS, with a specific focus on its principles, attitudes, and behaviours.

The articles gave more detail on challenges than the presentations and films, especially a learning paper by David and Mancini (2004). In this paper, they noted that 'the culture of some country programmes was (and, in some cases, remains) quite at odds with both ALPS and *Fighting Poverty Together*' (ibid., p. 12). They noted challenges for ALPS implementation such as high staff turnover and restrictive donor requirements. These and the other challenges are discussed further in later chapters of this book.

But despite this article describing these challenges, internal authors were generally very positive and hopeful about ALPS. For instance, David and Mancini (ibid., p. 9) noted in the same article:

ALPS breaks new ground. ALPS is different because it is an [international] NGO system which aspires to promote organisational adherence to much-vaunted rhetoric. Embedded in each of the core requirements of ALPS is the emphasis on process, the aim being to gradually transform the way ActionAid carries out its work. At each stage there is an emphasis on increasing transparency, participation, gender and power analysis, downward accountability, honesty and a genuine sharing of power in the development process.

However, the problem was, there was very little in these externally presented works about actual practice at community level. While there were some examples from country programmes in the articles and presentations that demonstrated how ALPS was operating in different countries, these were brief and the same anecdotes tended to be repeated from article to article and from presentation to presentation. Moreover, all the published articles used data from 2004 or earlier. Given that ALPS began in 2000, it would be assumed by the time I was looking into this in the late 2000s, that more examples of practice would have become available as the years progressed and as the system matured in country programmes. But there was an odd silence here. There was also no in-depth or longitudinal study in any of the published literature of how ALPS was operating in practice in any country.

Given this dearth of practice in the literature, the expositions of ALPS by ActionAid staff, particularly the presentations I attended, could again, like the external mentions, potentially give the impression that the introduction and existence of the system was an achievement in itself, rather than real achievement being based on how ALPS was actually operating in practice (Ferretti, 2007).

At the same time, I could see from documents and initial conversations that significant efforts had been made to implement ALPS internationally and at the level of different ActionAid country programmes over the years. For me, this implied there should be plenty to study.

I was keen to fill this gap by researching ALPS practice on the ground. Having reviewed other initiatives, I was convinced that ALPS was the most significant downward accountability initiative in the development NGO sector. I approached ActionAid for permission to study it, which the then-CEO granted. In the next chapter, I will discuss how I did my research and what I learnt.

CHAPTER SEVEN
What I learnt about ActionAid's accountability

I spent several years studying ActionAid at international, national, and community levels, focusing on a period of about 15 years from the late 1990s onward.[10]

At international level, I wanted to understand the big picture organisational perspective of the Accountability Learning and Planning System (ALPS). From 2008 to 2011, I conducted 22 interviews of current and former ActionAid staff and trustees in person in Johannesburg, Brighton, London, Nairobi, Accra, and Dublin, and by phone to New Zealand. I was fortunate to be travelling occasionally to Africa and Asia via the UK for work during this period, and since my research stretched over a number of years, I could eventually do almost all interviews in person, which helped to build rapport.

I also read documents about accountability in ActionAid at the international level and in various country programmes. This comprised (a whopping) 1,130 documents in all by the end of my research, produced between the mid-1990s and the end of 2012. These documents included strategies, reports, reviews, policies, meeting minutes, audits, staff surveys, and newsletters. Finally, I attended three workshops during which ActionAid staff discussed ALPS.

Researching at country level

The first issue I discussed with ActionAid after they agreed to my research was where to study ALPS practice. I knew I needed to be able to do research at the coalface at the community level to see if ALPS was making a difference there. So it made sense to hone in on one country to be able to look in depth, as well as looking at ALPS at the international level more broadly. Early interviews and reading that I did suggested that the implementation of ALPS varied significantly across ActionAid's country programmes.

I selected ActionAid Uganda as a country programme for particular focus. The main reason for this tied in with my overall desire to study an initiative on which considerable efforts had been expended so that, if it wasn't successful, the rationale wouldn't simply be that not much effort had been put in. ActionAid Uganda was seen within ActionAid globally as a model for ALPS practice in the early days of 2000–2003 (Okwaare and Chapman, 2006). It came up continuously in my early conversations with staff and former staff, as well as in my reading, with people noting that a lot had been invested in ALPS in Uganda. Hence, I knew there would be considerable information and data available on ALPS practice, much more than would be available in a country which had given little attention to the system.

Having spent the first couple of years of my research on the broader literature and on ActionAid International, I then spent five months in Uganda in 2011 and 2012. I was based initially at the ActionAid Uganda headquarters in Kampala, and then travelled to two districts in the east – Katakwi and Pallisa – on which I placed particular emphasis, as they were two districts in which ActionAid had worked throughout the entire period from the late 1990s onwards. I also undertook shorter visits to other ActionAid locations, such as Masindi, Apac, Kalangala, Kumi, and Bwaise.

I spent much of my time interviewing ActionAid staff and former staff; trustees; representatives from local partner organisations; government staff at both national and local level; and, critically, intended beneficiaries of ActionAid's work at community level. In total I conducted 100 interviews related to Uganda, almost all face-to-face, with the vast majority taking place within Uganda itself but with interviews also in London, New Delhi, and Nairobi with people who used to work with ActionAid Uganda.

The fairly significant length of my interviews – usually approximately one hour, but a minority significantly longer, up to four hours – assisted in building the trust that is so vital for frank discussions and reflection. I took care to balance between different types of stakeholders – people who were engaged during different time periods and who worked at different levels – to avoid a bias towards interviewing management.

Participant observation was a major part of my research at the Uganda level. Participant observation, a research method from ethnography, is based upon the rationale that, while interviews can be extremely informative on people's views, their words and actions are likely to differ, and thus it is also important to see what they actually do.[11] To understand the organisation through observation, I found it very important to participate in general meetings and events, not just those with an accountability focus. Thus, I attended meetings of management and staff, which were focused on areas such as programming, audit, and human resources. I participated in workshops for the new strategy formulation process at local and national levels and attended a programme staff retreat. In terms of informal interactions, I spent lots of time in cars with staff on the way to field visits, shared meals, and generally observed how staff interacted in the office and in the course of their field work. This was very useful to gain insights into the atmosphere within the organisation and the day-to-day issues that concern staff.

I also spent time with partners and communities in the various locations. Specifically on accountability, I attended seven (six local and one regional) participatory review and reflection process meetings (PRRPs), a key ALPS process that I will detail further later in this book. I also hunted around for transparency boards, another important tool of ALPS.

As part of my observation, I took photographs of events which I will include in later chapters.[12] The photographs proved more valuable than I expected them to be, as they capture the atmosphere of the settings of participatory approaches and the detail of transparency boards, which help to capture quality and provide an important complement to descriptions in words.

In total I reviewed 618 documents on ActionAid Uganda, comprising similar categories to the international documents mentioned earlier – plans, reports, reviews, policies, and so on. I went through many documents which were only available in hard copy, particularly from the local offices.

The final method I used was an anonymous survey, which was intended to supplement interviews and observation by seeking similar information from a more quantitative angle, asking 30 ActionAid Uganda staff to rank and score the implementation of ALPS principles and processes.

I found it very useful to triangulate between the different methods. For example, participant observation enhanced my subsequent interviews: when interviewees, such as ActionAid staff members, knew that I had witnessed ALPS processes already, I found that they were far less likely to try to talk them up and thus interviews appeared to move more quickly to the central issues. Different methods also helped deepen my understanding by giving me multiple perspectives on the same event, for instance I might observe a meeting at community level, subsequently interview some of the community members who participated in the meeting, to get their perspectives, and then see the event be written up in a progress report by staff.

I was fortunate to be given excellent access by ActionAid. Despite being an outsider and, what's more, a staff member of a donor agency, ActionAid gave me unhindered access to any individual I wanted to interview and any document I wanted to read. Their transparency and openness was both remarkable and commendable.

Overview of my findings on ALPS

Throughout the remainder of the book, I will be bringing out specific lessons from my research with ActionAid. Here I will give a brief high-level overview of my overall findings at the international level, to complement the Uganda-specific lessons to follow.

Looking across all the country programmes, mainly via interviews and documents, I reached three main conclusions about ALPS implementation: it was inconsistent, it was often ritualistic, and yet, there was a persistence of rhetoric about the implementation which portrayed ALPS practice as matching up with its aims.

The first theme in my findings was that ALPS implementation was 'patchy' (David and Mancini, 2004, p. 18). An external consultant reviewed ALPS in 2004, as part of the broader *Taking Stock 2* organisational review, and found that the implementation of ALPS was inconsistent (Guijt, 2004). There were some pockets of excellent practice, particularly around participatory planning, shared learning with stakeholders, financial transparency, and staff being open to critical reflection. However, Guijt (2004, p. iii) concluded that much progress was still to be made: 'ALPS is not yet being applied systemically or systematically within each country or across the countries, themes and functions. There are some critical gaps in the ALPS logic and in its implementation'.

A second review of ALPS in 2007, this time internally conducted, came to a similar conclusion, noting that some positive creative examples existed of putting ALPS principles into practice, but that these examples were still not widespread (ActionAid, 2007). This finding about the patchiness of ALPS implementation permeated my own review. There were strikingly few in-depth case studies available of ALPS practice of downward accountability by 2012, given that the system had been in place since 2000. Furthermore, there was much repetition of the examples provided in different documents. For instance, participatory budgeting in Guatemala featured frequently, as did social audit in Nepal, and financial transparency in Kenya (Chapman et al., 2003; David et al., 2006; Ical and Leon, 2009).

The inconsistency of implementation that emerged in the reviews and documents was also expressed by my interviewees. One former staff member said, 'In 2003...some were doing bits of ALPS, some not at all, some didn't get it, some still don't get it'. Another former staff member commented that there were 'just isolated examples of good practice, which didn't blossom and didn't flower'.

The second and related theme that emerged was that of ALPS implementation being ritualistic and not demonstrating the requisite principles. In the *Taking Stock 3* review of governance, human resources, and organisational development, Fowler and Crane (2010, p. 17) noted:

> The Accountability, Learning and Planning System (Alps) focuses on processes and values that emphasise learning, transparency and accountability. The mechanics of Alps processes are widely understood and practiced, though perhaps with insufficient consistency and quality. However, attention to its underlying principles and values is noted by many as problematic.

The internal review undertaken of ALPS in 2007 also raised a serious concern about the practice of principles. It noted that, despite commendable efforts within ActionAid to expose staff to ALPS:

> many staff are still not familiar with Alps ... There is far too much attention on the bureaucratic requirements of Alps, and insufficient attention to the principles. In particular, too much attention is put to the output – e.g. the plan or the report – rather

> than the process ... the poor quality of our plans and reports, our inability to be accountable to multiple stakeholders – is related to an insufficient attention to principles in process. (ActionAid, 2007, p. 3)

Similarly, while all my interviewees viewed the spirit of ALPS as laudable, many commented that its original spirit had been lost. Some interviewees talked about the way in which ALPS had become routine and automatic over time, with one former staff member reflecting: 'After a few years ALPS became part of the institution and devalued. Originally it had freshness and was revolutionary. Then it became part of the mainstream, a box you tick. Not something you think about'. Another staff member, working at regional level, commented on ALPS implementation, 'Most countries in the region are very weak ... ALPS is seen as imposed ... It has become a ritual to do a [Participatory Review and Reflection Process]'.

This assessment of implementation had remained fairly consistent since the first review of ALPS in 2004: ALPS processes were usually happening but, despite a few notable exceptions, there were serious question marks over the extent to which these processes in many countries matched up with ALPS principles. This led to the third and final theme that emerged from my overall review of ALPS internationally, that ActionAid's practice of downward accountability was often still described positively by ActionAid staff, even when realities did not appear to match it.

There were a number of examples in internal documentation that would leave a reader with the impression that downward accountability practice was more or less as per ActionAid's stated intentions. For instance, the *Rights to End Poverty* strategy stated that, 'The majority of our time and resources are spent on the poverty frontline and our staff and local partners have built long-term relationships of mutual trust and respect with many poor and excluded people' (ActionAid, 2005, p. 16). In their self-review for the *Taking Stock 3* global review, the ActionAid International Directors stated that, 'ActionAid is now increasingly recognised for its grassroots people centred development and acknowledged as a leader in downward accountability and transparency' (ActionAid, 2010c, p. 1).

On the other hand, many authors and internal interviewees expressed scepticism that ALPS implementation of downward accountability was going as well as was sometimes implied, and raised the issue of a disconnect between what ActionAid said and what ActionAid did. A former advisor commented to me that 'ActionAid talked more about ALPS than did it'. ActionAid's Risk Management Report for 2011 noted, 'In the last few years however, our rhetoric on accountability has not been matched with actions which leaves the organisation vulnerable to accusations of not walking the talk' (ActionAid, 2011b, p. 4).

These findings were largely mirrored by my in-depth study of ActionAid Uganda, and I will start looking at these lessons in the next chapter.

CHAPTER EIGHT
Who represents the community?

I will now look at some of the specific lessons that emerged from my field work in Uganda, the first being on the same topic of partnership, which was a key aspect of ActionAid's downward accountability strategy. I will start with a little background on the country programme.

ActionAid had started working in Uganda from a base in Kenya in 1982 to assist the country during and after the highly destructive war that ended in 1986 (Kabenge et al., 2005). By the late 1990s, ActionAid Uganda was undertaking major service delivery projects such as building schools and roads, with up to 200 staff at a time.

However, by that time, the development status of the country had significantly improved. What's more, new thinking had come into the development sector in Uganda and internationally in terms of partnership with local organisations, government's responsibility for development work, and citizens getting more engaged in demanding services from their governments (Okwaare and Chapman, 2006). In this context, and in the context of the aforementioned shift within ActionAid International, a new Indian Country Director, Meenu Vadera, started work in ActionAid Uganda in 1998 bringing with her many of these new ideas. This is when the period of my research focus begins.

One of the first changes that Meenu Vadera made after her arrival was to engage the country programme much more in partnership with local organisations. While partnerships had existed prior to the late 1990s, most had been focused on the sub-contracting of specific programme activities by ActionAid, rather than allowing partners autonomy for driving their own poverty reduction activities (ActionAid Uganda, 2000, p. 58). Meenu vastly increased the focus on the latter form of partnership. The organisation went from partnering with 56 partners in 1999, to 116 in 2000, and to almost 200 in 2001 (ActionAid Uganda, 2001, 2002).

However, in the mid-2000s, partner fraud began to be uncovered. The annual report in 2003 noted that 'working with partners has posed enormous challenges in the area of accountability for funds' (ActionAid Uganda, 2004, p. 47). It was estimated by one staff member working in finance at the time that fraud reached £50,000 (sterling) per year in the early 2000s from a budget of over £3,000,000 (ActionAid Uganda, 2005b).[13] The 2005 evaluation of the country programme spoke of 'rampant' fraud during the period 1999–2004 (Kabenge et al., 2005, p. 39).

When I asked ActionAid Uganda staff in interviews what had gone wrong, they cited the rush to take on partners in a context that wasn't ready, recalling the first lesson I discussed above on the importance of context analysis for partnership.

Interestingly, staff members also raised the issue of representativeness, reporting that many of the initial partners were created simply to receive funds from ActionAid, rather than being pre-existing organisations representing poor people.

My own research, including watching partners interact with local communities in various meetings, found that this was still an issue for some of ActionAid's partners in the first half of the 2010s, which leads me to the third lesson of this book.

Lesson 3: Be careful who represents the local community in partnership or other localisation initiatives, and monitor how these groups are interacting with the wider group of community members.

The shift to partnership in ActionAid Uganda could have had the effect of being conducive to downward accountability, in that it could have reduced the distance between ActionAid and its intended beneficiaries by bringing in locally representative organisations to amplify the voices of community members. This was certainly the theory and the hoped-for scenario when Meenu Vadera ramped up partnership so significantly. However, I found that the way in which partnership evolved within ActionAid Uganda had, in many cases, the opposite effect of working against downward accountability. A key point here was a lack of representativeness and questionable constituencies of partners. I delved into this issue in interviews with staff members and partners and by reviewing documents about partnership within the organisation.

Naturally, the first indicator that some partners did not represent the wider community was the instances of partner fraud. These emerged in the early 2000s as I mentioned above, but this was still a very live issue during my research in the 2010s as I will come back to later. Similar to the case study of fraud in Concern's partner in South Sudan, it was clear that the partner organisation did not represent the local community at times when money was being taken by the leadership for personal gain.

Many staff members in interviews with me were critical of partners' downward accountability. One former staff member noted, 'Partners are not very accountable [to communities]. They are dealing with survival, thinking: "how can ActionAid fund me?"'

Staff members often commented that partners only consulted leaders in the community, rather than the wider community which they claimed to represent. In a survey I conducted of staff, one wrote in a section on 'participation of poor people in reviews and planning' that the 'participation of the poor is limited to partner organisation level while the expectation is for them to consult further, this doesn't in reality happen. If [it] does, it's still those who're well off and influen[tial] whose opinions are sought'. Documents suggested that this was not a new issue. For example, partner self-assessments conducted in 2005 found that 90 per cent of partners only did participation with community leaders (ActionAid Uganda, 2005a).

But interestingly, partners I spoke to also reported that they struggled to get community participation if they could not provide financial incentives. One partner staff member in Katakwi complained that without allowances, even the organisation's board members did not show up for meetings: 'People don't come to meetings if they don't think there'll be food and transport refund. [The chairperson] tried to hold the meeting but few people showed up. They expect an allowance. When there was a meeting in March only six members came from 23'.

In areas with high poverty levels in which ActionAid works, this was perhaps understandable and not surprising. However, it did not lend credence to how these partners are described by ActionAid. For instance, in annual reports, there was a partner classification table which used the terminology 'Representative

Structures of the Poor and Excluded People and Right Holders' (ActionAid Uganda, 2013, p. 32).

Having gotten this impression of problems with the representativeness of some partners from my document review and interviews, I decided to see for myself at community level how interactions were between partners and community members.

Observation of participatory processes

My best opportunity to observe this relationship was during six PRRPs that I attended. These were run by different partner organisations at the request of ActionAid in two different parts of the country. The PRRP was a core process set out in ALPS to enhance participation and transparency of ActionAid and its partners. The purpose of PRRPs was to work with stakeholder and community groups to:

- assess what has been done;
- what has been learnt;
- and, within this analysis, articulate what will be done differently in the future. (ActionAid, 2006a, p. 27)

According to ALPS, PRRPs were intended to be periodic meetings with community members, partners, and other stakeholders whereby consultation and learning takes place in a manner which is empowering for community members, and which increases ActionAid's accountability and transparency to these groups. As per the ALPS principles, these sessions should also promote an analysis of power and work towards a transformation of power dynamics to give priority to poor and marginalised people, particularly women (ActionAid, 2006a).

In practice, in Uganda during my research, community-level PRRPs were taking place on a regular basis in the Local Rights Programmes (LRPs) at least once a year, often twice. From my observation of six community-level PRRPs in two different districts, these were occasions during which partners and community members and often, but not always, ActionAid staff, discussed issues related to ongoing programming and often, but not always, discussed plans for the future. Thus, they provided a forum for consultation and transparency, and an opportunity for the views of community members to feed into the decisions of ActionAid and partners. These were the positives.

Photo 8.1 Participants at PRRP in Acanga, Katakwi LRP, 23 July 2011

However, I invariably observed that the quality of these PRRPs was low as compared with the intention. None of the sessions I attended gave me a positive impression of how partners were interacting with communities. In all PRRPs, there was a hierarchical tone between the partners and the community members. In each of the sessions, the set-up was similar to a school setting with the partner representatives and ActionAid staff (if present) seeming like teachers at the top of the room, and the community members as students. The photograph above and the two below from Katakwi District, illustrate this set-up (the second and third photos are of the same scene from different angles). Three of the six PRRPs which I attended did, in fact, take place in school buildings, but in no case was there any attempt by ActionAid or the partner to make any adjustments to the room set-up in order to create a more egalitarian arrangement (see Photos 8.1 and 8.2).

The physical distance between the partner and ActionAid staff, and the members of the community, as can be seen in Photo 8.3, also has metaphorical significance as it represented the lack of connection or empathy between the partner and the community members that was evident throughout the session. I found that

Photo 8.2 Participants at PRRP in Kapujan, Katakwi LRP, 25 July 2011

Photo 8.3 Facilitators at PRRP in Kapujan, Katakwi LRP, 25 July 2011

partners were generally respectful and friendly in their facilitation, but in this particular PRRP, facilitation was harsh and commanding. The partner representative spent a lot of time berating community members for their poor attendance, to which they responded that there was a funeral taking place in the next village. This type of facilitation obviously militates against the PRRP as a learning or empowering process.

In the PRRP shown in Photo 8.1, the facilitation was more friendly, but the PRRP nevertheless consisted of a lecture by the head of the partner organisation. This goes against the guideline in ALPS that 'involvement of poor and excluded people along with donors and other stakeholders requires very sensitive facilitating so that all feel comfortable to contribute' (ActionAid, 2006a, p. 27).

The atmosphere of the PRRPs did not suggest that the partner organisation was driven by the views of this community, or that the partner organisations were *representatives* of this community.

Delving more into representativeness

We need to be very careful in localisation efforts to understand what we mean by *local*, who comprises *the community*, and who represents whom. This applies whether we are working through a partnership model or trying to localise in other ways. Unfortunately, there are no easy answers to these difficult questions, but it is critical that they are asked. Every NGO and donor will then need to decide whether or not the answers to these questions and their subsequent programming plans help them to reach their localisation objectives.

Two dimensions are particularly important to consider:

1. Who is claiming to have knowledge of the needs of the community and speaking on their behalf?
2. How are these community interlocutors seeking input from the wider community members on an ongoing basis?

We often use the term 'the community' for convenience, but obviously there is nothing uniform or unitary about any group of people who simply happen to live in the same locality. Often NGOs are established by educated middle-class professionals, which makes sense given the requirements to liaise with donors, fill in proposals, and so on. Do these individuals know about and represent the poorest and most marginalised groups in a community which are often the target group of the NGO or donor? Are there issues of tribal or ethnic divisions? Is there any neglect of women's perspectives? These are not new questions – this is Participation 101! But it is nevertheless important that they be asked each and every time local partners or other interlocutors are being selected with the understanding that they have the potential to represent a particular community.

Second, at times, international NGOs and donors assume that if they are working in partnership with a local NGO that they do not have to worry about the issue of participation and accountability to communities as the local NGO will already be close to the communities where they work. That box will automatically be ticked! As I have seen numerous times over the years in my work and in my research, this can often be a faulty assumption.

The local partner NGOs simply may not prioritise the participation of, or accountability to, others in the community. They may feel that they have a good handle on the poverty situation in the area. 'We *are* the community' is a common refrain I have heard throughout my work over the years when I have asked local partners about community participation. They therefore feel it would not be useful to ask others questions to which they feel they already have the answer.

Engaging in quality participation is difficult and time-consuming. International actors should not wash their hands of the issue of participation because it has been contracted to a local organisation, but should work with their local partners in a concerted manner to make sure that this occurs effectively.

What's most important here, in my view, is for NGOs and donors to figure out what they want to achieve with their localisation agenda and then try to ensure that the local actors they seek to work with will help achieve this. It's important to do this without prior assumptions about the local community being in any way homogeneous.

As may be becoming evident here, I am suggesting that donors or NGOs wanting to localise need to spend more time asking questions and understanding what is appropriate in different contexts. This links to the next lesson which is about the implications of this approach for staffing.

CHAPTER NINE
Staffing for localisation

Localisation is sometimes seen as inevitably reducing the staffing requirements of international organisations. However, this might not be the case, at least initially. Doing localisation well needs an adequate quantity and type of staff, and what's adequate will (again!) depend on the context.

Lesson 4: Providing strong support to localisation will have implications for the quantity and types of staff of international organisations.

In my study of ActionAid Uganda, I found that staffing was a key obstacle to ALPS being implemented well. There were issues of staff being overloaded, as well as the types of staff being recruited, which I will discuss here.

Quantity of staff time

As discussed earlier, the international *Fighting Poverty Together* strategy from 1999 led to a shift in ActionAid to working in partnership with far more local organisations. This also led to major restructuring within country programmes to reduce numbers of staff. In Uganda, from 202 staff members in 1994, numbers dropped to 142 in 2000, and to 99 in 2003 (ActionAid Uganda, 1994, 2001, 2004). This reduction in staff took place alongside the increase in partners from 56 in 1999 to almost 200 in 2001 (ActionAid Uganda, 2001, 2002).

However, this reduction in staff did not appear to take into account the high number of partners, or their low capacity level, or the sheer volume of work involved in quality capacity building.

On the positive side, some partners praised the training they received from ActionAid. My in-depth review of documentation on Katakwi District since the late 1990s pointed to several phases of assessments and capacity building initiatives for partners. Although interviewees also made the point that ActionAid support to partners tended to be centred on finance and audit issues, rather than programming.

Generally, however, my findings on ActionAid Uganda's support to partners were negative, concluding that there was inadequate time spent supporting partners on areas like community engagement. This led to situations I saw myself in Uganda, with inexperienced partners leading participatory processes, poorly supported by over-stretched ActionAid staff. This reminded me of what I had read in an internal review at the international level:

> Despite the language of downward accountability, in reality, AAI [ActionAid International], in an attempt to work at a scale, is not structured to deeply engage with people at the grassroots level. We have over the past five years expanded at such a rate that we have a very high ratio of partners to staff, and of villages to partner. We do not have enough capacity at local level to really build the capacity of partners or community leaders to deal with difficult issues of power that come up around transparency and accountability, except in a few countries. (IASL, 2010, p. 5)

An illustration of this was provided at an internal workshop that I attended in Brighton on ALPS and accountability in ActionAid, this time in relation to ActionAid Nepal. An international staff member I spoke to at that workshop stated, 'There are 247 communities that are worked with and many partners. What does this mean for ongoing processes? ... ActionAid Nepal staff are overloaded. One staff might be supporting 10–20 organisations'. This issue exemplified the tendency, as phrased by one ActionAid staff member, for 'engagement to be 30 miles wide and half an inch deep' (ActionAid, 2006b, p. 3).

In Uganda, the lack of time ActionAid staff had to support or monitor partners, including around their use of participatory approaches, was one of the key complaints partner organisations made to me during interviews. This was particularly a problem as so many of the partners were nascent and weak. One partner commented to me, 'AA has a lean/skeleton staff...They don't have time to support partners, they are stretched'.

Therefore, in addition to the representativeness issue I mentioned above, lack of capacity building of partners for conducting Participatory Review and Reflection Processes (PRRP) appears to have fed into the problematic facilitation.

One staff member in Uganda made this point about the lack of staff time compromising participation or transparency processes: 'Staff are completely stretched. We are killing the processes and intentions by being stretched ... There are guidelines for PRRPs ... a preparation document, but people will say: when do I have the time to look at this?'

The 2010 evaluation of ActionAid Uganda noted that staff members were too busy for empowerment work. As another review found: '[ActionAid Uganda] staff seem to be busy with activities and routine work that they may not be able to spend adequate time on facilitating ... empowerment and transformation processes' (Kithinji et al., 2010, p. 19).

This point about inadequate support to partners had been consistently raised since 2000, when the vast increase in partners and vast reduction in staff numbers began. For instance, in an internal audit of the Katakwi Local Rights Programme (LRP) in 2006, data showed that contrary to the aim of visiting each partner twice a month, at best, one partner was visited every two to three months, and one partner was not visited at all in 18 months (ActionAid Uganda, 2006).

So what were staff spending their time on? Two areas stood out in Uganda: internal administrative tasks and administering child sponsorship. As one interviewee, an LRP staff member, commented, 'The two things that take time are sponsorship and procedures. You spend so much time on procedures, not mindful of outcome'.

My research strongly suggested a significant amount of staff time was spent on administrative tasks. One staff member commented, '[LRP] managers complain about overwork but it seems to be mostly on administrative work, not programme work. They are not analysing data or making projections. They are doing accountabilities and preparing for the auditor'. The 2010 evaluators noted that, 'there are too many systems and policies in place ... AAIU [ActionAid International Uganda] has become over bureaucratic' (Kithinji et al., 2010, p. 68).

However, the focus on these administrative tasks was not accidental; it had emerged in part from a significant number of instances of fraud among staff, as well as partners over the years. These controls were defended by some staff members I interviewed on the basis of the high prevalence of corruption. One said, 'Without controls, AA would have gone under. Controls have to remain. It depends on culture. People can work as a team to be corrupt. If you remove one control ... In the environment people survive by stealing, there needs to be a strong deterrent'.

While there were different views on how necessary the controls were, it was clear that the procedures took up much staff time, in a context where staff time was already seen to be extremely limited.

The second area which took up a lot of staff time was fulfilling sponsorship requirements. ActionAid's funds were raised largely from members of the public in the UK, who sponsored children within the communities in which ActionAid worked, in that they contributed a monthly amount in a particular child's name. ActionAid Uganda's income in 2011 was 55 per cent from sponsorship – from approximately 19,000 individual sponsors (ActionAid Uganda, 2012b).

Staff constantly spoke of the burdensome child sponsorship requirements. I found in my time at local level that a significant amount of priority was given to fulfilling child sponsorship requirements, such as photos of children and letters. On one field visit with a programme officer, I noticed that she appeared far more concerned with ensuring that photos were taken of particular sponsored children, than with the quality of the subsequent PRRP. One interviewee noted, 'Child sponsorship is non-negotiable. If there are queries you have to drop everything else'.

Thus, tasks around administration and sponsorship were being prioritised and others relating to community engagement were not being adequately carried out.[14] Community-level work seemed consistently to be either rushed, such as the PRRPs I attended, or neglected. Interestingly, I noticed that within the PRRPs, the procedure of filling in attendance sheets, on which the customary soda and biscuit distribution was based, was a high priority that took a lot of staff and participant attention away from the PRRP proceedings. Similarly, one partner spoke of ActionAid staff spending all their time on field visits 'filling vouchers'.

The lack of time given to community engagement may also have related to the performance of some staff in the organisation, rather than just staffing numbers.[15] However, at least part of the issue here was excess workload. Overload of ActionAid staff was constantly mentioned by interviewees, both inside and outside of the organisation. It was also a major theme throughout my observation in ActionAid Uganda.

Thus, quantity of staff for localisation needs to be considered and also how staff are prioritising and deciding how to use their available time. And of course organisations have a huge role here; clearly, for ActionAid, the incentives in place were not leading staff to prioritise participation or transparency processes or support to partners for these.

Quality and types of staff

The quality and types of staff was a point raised even more strongly than quantity by interviewees. The *Taking Stock 3* review of ActionAid International found that there were shortcomings in the principles and values of ALPS practice, and noted: 'In part this relates to the quality and skill of frontline staff on the ground' (Fowler and Crane, 2010, p. 17). In my analysis, how staff were recruited, and the induction and training provided by ActionAid on ALPS and related processes were both problematic.

On the first of these two issues, numerous international interviewees spoke of a shift, from the introduction of the human rights-based approach in the late 1990s, to the recruitment and promotion of staff who could write and speak well in policy fora, rather than those who could work well with communities and partners. Kate Newman (2011, p. 262), a former staff member, noted in her PhD study of the human rights-based approach within ActionAid that, 'ActionAid had inadvertently excluded the voices of those to whom it strove to be most accountable. The gap existed in part because of the emphasis at the recruitment stage where policy and advocacy skills were being stressed, over and above experience in programme development and community participation'.

Indeed the predominant view of interviewees was that there had been a tendency to recruit the wrong type of staff for community-level work. A former staff member at international level recalled, '[Salil Shetty – former CEO] recruited activists ... there was a move to not valuing community development skills'. Another staff member commented, 'people are being hired on paper qualifications, not for values and learning spirit – staff have lost the skills for participatory processes'.

This was very much borne out in Uganda.

Programme officers at LRP level had the primary responsibility for liaising with communities and with partner organisations, a critical role for an organisation prioritising downward accountability. However, programme officers were not always well-placed for this role which, in part, related to how they were recruited and the nature of their jobs, and in part, as is discussed below, how they were trained within ActionAid.

One staff member commented that programme officers:

> have to do [human resources], procurement, the monthly financial report. Audit, sponsorship work. In one head there are many small things. For projects there will be proposals. It's not about capacity, it's about demands. All have high importance. There's [Impact Assessment and Shared Learning], finance, accountabilities … At the [LRP] level, there's finance, admin, [human resources], communication, [information communication technology], sponsorship grants, partnership, audit, programme development manager. Then there are demands from the government and the community … There may be donor visits, there are meetings. You can't think straight.

While the point that this staff member was making related to an overload of demands in terms of time, it is easy to see how an organisation might struggle to recruit for these diverse tasks in terms of skills. Inevitably, in the recruitment process for such a wide array of tasks, prioritisation is needed. When I looked into this, I found that there was no community-related experience required in the job specification for this role. An illustration of this was the fact that the programme officers in one of the local areas I visited did not speak the regional language, which was the main language of the communities to which they were assigned. I found this very surprising, and it did suggest a lack of prioritisation of community work for that role as against more administrative tasks.

Coming to the second issue, many interviewees at the international level spoke of the lack of induction and support given to staff to embody the principles and behaviours required by ALPS, and to deal with difficult areas of culture and power dynamics that arise in participatory work. Similarly, the 2007 ALPS review noted, 'Embedding Alps requires more than training on "how to" – it requires transforming attitudes and behaviours, unlearning traditional ways of managing programmes. It requires changing organizational culture to create an enabling environment' (ActionAid, 2007, p. 3).

The same review found that many staff members did not have an adequate understanding of ALPS and that 'much more work' was required on attitudes and behaviours (ibid., p. 19).

In the late 2000s, there was a decision to invest more of the capacity of the Impact Assessment and Shared Learning Unit at headquarters into capacity building of staff for ALPS, particularly to enhance learning and the quality and consistency of ALPS processes, and ActionAid's multiple accountabilities more broadly. However, interviewees, including those from that Unit, did not see this as adequate.

A similar picture emerged in Uganda when it came to induction and training on approaches and skill sets related to downward accountability. There were clear weaknesses in the skills and/or the will of ActionAid and partners to facilitate quality participatory processes.

Investment in capacities for participation was said to have declined with the shift to the human rights-based approach. It is notable that the skills gap in participatory approaches was recognised by the organisation, which led to a two-week training course in January 2011 for ActionAid staff. During this training course, staff expressed the need for considerable further trainings.

A final problem that arose relating to the issue of staff quality for downward accountability was that of high staff turnover, which of course erodes the value of trainings done and any work done on staff attitudes and behaviours. I will come back to turnover in a later chapter.

Thus, it is clear that challenges in the recruitment of staff, and in the induction and training of staff and partners contributed to weaknesses in ActionAid's downward accountability.

The key point here is that supporting localisation, even when the focus is on implementing through partners, may need a significant allocation of the staff time of international organisations, depending of course on the partners and the context. It will not necessarily be a way to save staff costs as is often assumed, at least not in the short term. It is certainly the case, however, that a different skill set is needed to support localisation from what was needed for direct implementation, and this skill set needs to be deliberately recruited for or built.

In an illustration of how complex localisation dynamics can be, and why adequate quality staff are needed, in the next chapter, I will look at the centrality of power dynamics within communities and within NGOs themselves for downward accountability.

CHAPTER TEN
The centrality of power dynamics

I realised at a certain stage in my research on ActionAid that a lot of issues came down to power dynamics. When we are trying to prioritise the poorest and most vulnerable community members, we are, by definition, working against the grain of hierarchies within communities. Partners were often towards the top of this hierarchy. I had found in the work that I did with Concern that partner organisations I worked with were generally led by elites, some of whom were deeply politically connected.[16]

One example from my observation of Participatory Review and Reflection Processes (PRRPs) stuck with me. Photo 10.1 shows a group work exercise in Gogonyo in Pallisa Local Rights Programme (LRP). The exercise was for the groups to feed back views on what ActionAid should prioritise going forward. This exercise quickly divided into the younger, more educated, male and female leaders of the partner organisation (standing) and the older, female community members, seemingly less educated and less well off (sitting). The subsequent presentation then comprised the views of the younger group. The ActionAid staff present did not comment in any way on this division – in fact, they appeared not to notice.

Lesson 5: Addressing power dynamics at community level and within NGOs themselves is central to localisation. Understanding these dynamics is a critical first step to improvements.

There is quite a bit of focus on the centrality of power in the NGO literature. Lewis (2007, p. 144), in a case study of accountability in a Bangladeshi NGO, points to context and culture as key to understanding accountability issues within NGOs as, 'NGO structures, activities and relationships are socially embedded

Photo 10.1 Group work during PRRP in Gogonyo, Pallisa LRP, 13 July 2011

within institutions and power structures at both local and international levels'.

Soon after the creation of the Accountability Learning and Planning System (ALPS), ActionAid had recognised the difficulties in transforming power, even its own power as an organisation, to achieve the goal of downward accountability in ALPS. For instance, David and Mancini (2003, p. 7) noted in a conference presentation on ALPS that 'ActionAid is a large International NGO which is changing constantly, which has a huge power vis-à-vis many of its partners and which (in places) has a very dominant hierarchy. As such, there is an inherent contradiction when ActionAid is trying to open up space for honest feedback and criticism'.

This perspective aligns with the scepticism of authors such as Najam (1996), Cooke and Kothari (2001), and Williams (2010), regarding the lack of effectiveness of participatory mechanisms in the context of power imbalances between NGOs and beneficiaries. However, despite this awareness existing within ActionAid, my research shows that power dynamics at community level were still a serious obstacle to its downward accountability.

One of the key tenets of ALPS was that its processes should be used to promote awareness and confidence in community members to hold ActionAid and its partners to account, and that this would help to transform power relationships (ActionAid, 2006a). However, as academics Ebrahim and Weisband (2007, p. 19) pointed out in a book reviewing accountability dynamics in modern organisations, in practice, accountability processes will, in fact, tend to reinforce existing power dynamics: 'Accountability is a social phenomenon, reflective of relationships of power in society. One can thus expect the instruments of accountability to reproduce those relationships rather than overturn them'.

Power dynamics between ActionAid, partners, and community members

Similarly, I found that power dynamics between ActionAid and its partners and community members were deep-rooted and generally unfavourable to prospects of downward accountability. My observation at field level showed a hierarchical relationship between ActionAid and community members, with little evidence of the community challenging the organisation.

The downward accountability envisioned in ALPS requires two power transformations. First, ActionAid staff members and partners should voluntarily 'reverse' their power relationships vis-à-vis community members (Chambers, 1996). Second, community members should simultaneously demand greater levels of accountability from ActionAid staff and partners. Neither of these two transformations was apparent in my case study to any significant degree. I found, in fact, that both transformations are extremely challenging and go against the status quo in countries such as Uganda, where educated and higher status persons, and particularly those who are responsible for resources, such as NGO workers, are automatically deferred to within society. In addition, these people often act in a way that befits their perceived status.

There were some ALPS processes which aimed to address voluntary reversal, such as PRRPs with communities which provided opportunities for critique and feedback. However, as my findings on PRRPs in Uganda and at international level suggested, the quality of these processes was often poor. Rather than the vibrant processes envisioned by ALPS, what I observed were fairly ritualistic processes of consultation wherein community members were asked for input on desired project activities, this was noted down on flipchart papers, and these were then taken away for ActionAid and the partner to decide upon at a later stage.

There were several examples of poor behaviour by ActionAid and partners towards community members, as I mentioned above. For instance, some partners openly lectured community members during PRRPs. In addition, at three of the six PRRPs I attended, there were complaints by participants about the short notice and unsuitability of the timing. In Buseeta in Pallisa LRP, for example, participants said that, due to the agricultural season, most of the 200 community members involved with ActionAid could not make the PRRP, particularly as they had only learnt about the session the previous day.

However, in most cases relationships between staff, partners, and community members appeared cordial and respectful. Yet despite largely friendly relationships, the prevalent hierarchy was maintained without any evident efforts to change it.

The second intended power transformation was similarly not in evidence. During participatory processes, despite the fact that complaints were often made that community members had not received particular project inputs, or that inputs had arrived too late, I did not observe any real challenge to ActionAid or partners. One interviewee in Uganda commented, 'It's a reflection of Ugandan culture which is to never question your parents, your teacher, (generally) the president'.

When I asked community members in Katakwi whether they ever asked other NGOs to share budget information with them, such as the information they had received from the ActionAid partner during a PRRP, the response was simply, 'No'. One man added, 'The vulnerable we don't have power, we fear that assistance will be withdrawn'.

This echoes the findings of the case study by Agyemang et al. (2009, p. 30) which looked at the effectiveness of NGO accountability mechanisms in Ghana. The case study found that the poverty and vulnerability of beneficiaries created a fear which prevented them from questioning the NGO. The same point was raised by an interviewee with respect to partners' participation in an ActionAid meeting being constrained by their fear of management, such that they were on their 'Sunday best'.

A striking example of this lack of questioning of ActionAid by community members, from the international dimension of my case study, was that of social audit in Nepal. Social audit in Nepal was often lauded within ActionAid as one of the best examples of ALPS practice (ActionAid, 2010a). Social audit, as defined by ActionAid Nepal, was similar to the PRRP called for within ALPS: it was a session with partners, intended beneficiaries, and government actors to present current programming work, including the budget, and to seek feedback on performance (ActionAid Nepal, 2010).

Social audit had been much praised by international reviewers based on a lot of positive features such as ActionAid's transparency during the sessions. However, internal reports in ActionAid Nepal found that community members were not asking critical questions of ActionAid within the process, which was at the very heart of what the process was supposed to comprise. As an ActionAid Nepal study of ALPS in three districts found, community members 'hardly recall a moment when they questioned the rationale or the relevance of any particular programme or budget allocated to them' (ActionAid Nepal, 2006, p. 9). An internal case study by ActionAid Nepal a few years later had similar findings. While the case study noted that there were certainly positive aspects to the social audit process, particularly around creating a culture of transparency that had ripple effects to other organisations, some significant weaknesses were identified, most remarkably, 'We have not been able to encourage participants to give honest and critical feedback. It is important to ensure that the process does not end up becoming a back-slapping exercise' (ActionAid Nepal, 2010, p. 2).

The key point here is that, even in the best-case scenario, if an organisation such as ActionAid Nepal is making significant efforts to be transparent and accountable, various barriers such as community members' dependant position, lack of confidence of community members to be honest and frank with ActionAid staff or partners, or other cultural factors, may prevent community members from taking advantage of this. Power dynamics cannot be easily wished away.

Taking a broader perspective on participatory approaches in Africa, Imam (2010, p.12) noted in a global review of ActionAid that:

> many of those AA works with would simply not wish to 'bite the hand that feeds' as they see AA as a provider, rather than a

partner with which they have an equal and mutually beneficial relationship. In addition, many (especially at [LRP] level) likened AA to a parent – in many African cultures it is simply not done to criticise parents openly and to their faces. Participatory techniques need to be very carefully understood and used if they are to address these issues and engage in real reflection and analysis.

Thus, the reluctance to challenge ActionAid or its partners was evident at international level, as well as in my study of Uganda, and belied hopes of communities demanding accountability.

Organisational hierarchy within NGOs

Another relevant dimension here is power dynamics within ActionAid itself. I found that staff members had a tendency to follow the leader regardless of their own views and beliefs.[17] This was also strongly related to personal livelihood concerns, which become more acute at lower levels of the organisation. Often it is these lower-level staff, for example field staff, who are best placed to comment on the realities of practice, but they may be the least empowered to do so.[18]

Newman (2011, p. 253) found that the relationship between local staff and partners, and national staff members in ActionAid, tended to consist of a one-way, upward flow of information and noted, 'Given this dynamic it is unlikely that local staff or those working in partner organisations would communicate local realities 'up the system' unless directly asked for input'. This resonates with one of Guijt's findings in her 2004 ALPS review. She found that lower-level staff had very insightful critical views on ALPS, but they were unable to turn their insights into improvements.

My research suggested that a hierarchical culture within Uganda and within Ugandan NGOs had led to ActionAid staff tending to fall in line with the leadership on new approaches or systems over the years, even if they did not agree with them. A former staff member commented, 'There is also a Ugandan thing to sense the direction of leadership. When people don't agree, they are not so candid, they don't express reservations. If you voice concerns, it looks like you're resisting change'.

While the quality of ALPS practices was weak according to my observation, field staff did not appear to be exposing this fact. Most of them admitted it to me in interviews, although usually only after they knew that I had already observed the practices myself. Given the fact that approaches such as ALPS were mandatory within the organisation, frontline staff members had incentives to feed into the image that they are being implemented well, rather than pointing out weaknesses.

The upshot for power dynamics

A major effort would be required to make progress on transforming power relationships to promote accountability of ActionAid to its intended beneficiaries, given all the inherent obstacles I have mentioned. Yet, it did not seem that ActionAid was well set up at the time of my research to promote the intended power transformations.

The kinds of obstacles that I mentioned earlier such as overloaded staff, capacity gaps of partners, and prioritisation of administrative procedures and sponsorship work, militated against the intensive and long-term processes that would be needed to work on these deep-seated power issues. One interviewee spoke of the 'impatience' of ActionAid, as opposed to the long time periods needed for real change to occur. This recalls the earlier quotation from the self-review of the team responsible for accountability and related matters in ActionAid: 'We do not have enough capacity at local level to really build the capacity of partners or community leaders to deal with difficult issues of power that come up around transparency and accountability, except in a few countries' (IASL, 2010, p. 5).

Thus, in practice, power dynamics at community level and between communities, partners, and ActionAid emerged as a major barrier to NGO accountability to intended beneficiaries. And power dynamics within ActionAid made it less likely that field staff would speak up about the real challenges they faced.

In the next chapter, I will expand on the concept of ActionAid's 'impatience' and discuss the impact of NGOs jumping from trend to trend.

CHAPTER ELEVEN
Trend-jumping

My research illustrated the tendency of ActionAid leaders to introduce new approaches and strategies on a regular basis. One of my interviewees in Uganda used the term 'trend-jumping' to describe this. In this chapter, I focus on how the practice of constantly changing approaches negatively affected the success of initiatives such as ALPS, as it does NGO localisation initiatives more broadly.

At the international level in ActionAid, interviewees spoke, usually critically, of the organisation's constant shifts of approach. Former staff member Newman (2011, p. 104), in her study of ActionAid's work on rights and participation, cited an interviewee who, when asked to describe ActionAid in less than five words based on her experience with the organisation in the 1990s, said, 'Continuously restructuring and restructuring'. In ActionAid's external stakeholder review for *Taking Stock 3*, one respondent noted that the organisation was 'high on initiatives, low on follow through. Too many flavour-of-season management initiatives' (Leach, 2010, p. 20).

Similarly, it was evident in my research that many change processes had taken place in ActionAid Uganda since 1998, including an organisational development process, the shift to partnership and the human rights-based approach, new strategies with new themes and campaigns, changes in the governance structure, a new monitoring framework, and innovations in sponsorship to name just a few. Many interviewees in Uganda were critical of what they viewed as changes due to 'fads' and 'repackaging', particularly in relation to what were seen as the sudden shifts to partnership and the human rights-based approach. One interviewee complained, 'The speed in AA is too much. A pilot can be a success but AA has lost interest and is now looking for a newer model. There is no grounding it'.

Lesson 6: The NGO tendency for trend-jumping undermines the potential for localisation; NGOs need to stay the course.

Trend-jumping is far from being an issue unique to ActionAid. A World Vision staff member in Zimbabwe, cited by Bornstein (2005, p. 70) in her study of the organisation, stated, 'The only thing constant here is change'.

Sometimes trend-jumping is linked in the literature to the effects of managerialism, which has been a major influence on the international NGO sector, particularly in the early 2000s, and which is related to a much increased focus on results (Wallace et al., 2007; Shutt, 2009). Managerialism is said to be characterised by 'a relatively uncritical acceptance of corporate management in all administrative contexts' (Gulrajani, 2011, p. 9). It has increasingly influenced NGO practice since the 1980s.

Authors writing about managerialist practices within NGOs often describe a tendency toward new fads and trends, encouraged by a regular turnover of staff. The tendency towards fads is referred to by David Sogge (1996, p. 16), an author on development NGOs, as the 'continuity of discontinuity'. This is accompanied by what Lewis (2013) describes as the propensity of new staff to dismiss the work of their predecessors and start afresh in order to make their mark, hence reducing the prospects for organisational learning. Indeed, these two enabling factors of staff turnover and the dismissal of predecessors' work came out strongly in my research in Uganda.

Staff turnover

In Uganda, turnover was an issue constantly raised by interviewees and in documentation. It was noted in the 2011 internal audit report of the country programme, that turnover in ActionAid Uganda in 2011 was 25 per cent, from a staff of 78 (ActionAid Uganda, 2012a). The report further noted that '[ActionAid Uganda] has had considerable staff turnover in 2011, including some of the most senior positions in the organisation. In the past 12 months there have been three different Internal Audit Managers and three different Programme Directors. The longest serving CMT

[Country Management Team] members have been on the CMT for only two years' (ibid., p. 9).

Turnover was not a new issue in ActionAid Uganda. In the final report of an organisational development consultancy for ActionAid Uganda in 2003, UK academic Tina Wallace noted that the 'constant need to recruit and induct new senior staff has had a negative effect on the energy and motivation available for doing the work needed to transform [ActionAid Uganda]' (Wallace and Kaplan, 2003, p. 23). Interviewees made similar points to me in 2011 and 2012.

While different causes of turnover were posited by interviewees, there was a consensus in my research that the consistently high rate of turnover over the years in ActionAid Uganda had huge and negative implications for programme quality, including learning and relationships with partners and government.[19] High turnover was also seen to erode the value of trainings and any work done on staff attitudes and behaviours. Thus, initiatives such as ALPS were bound to suffer the consequences.

Lewis (2013, pp. 116–117) adds an additional element while speaking of the 'relentless emphasis on novelty and change' that characterises managerialism and also helps to maintain it: he speaks of the fact that expatriate staff of NGOs, often comprising the NGO management, are frequently on short-term contracts and are less likely to learn enough in this time to deeply question the status quo.

Abandoning predecessors' approaches

The second problematic factor that accompanies trend-jumping is the tendency of leaders, in this case country directors, to abandon the approaches of their predecessors without sufficient consideration. Lewis (2013, p. 117) talks about this, noting that:

> The bureaucratic logic within many agencies also tends to create incentives for a new appointee to a particular position to show their effectiveness by deliberately downplaying the ideas and work of their immediate predecessor, and beginning new work as a way to demonstrate their own particular 'added value'. The result may be the unnecessary development of

new initiatives, terms, and approaches in a process that further contributes to the suppression of past experiences and restricted learning.

This abandonment of predecessors' approaches was a strong theme in my interviews in Uganda. It was illustrated by one former senior staff member to me in an interview, referring to a series of country directors from the late 1990s to the mid-2000s:[20]

From Anthony to Meenu there was a change, from Meenu to Amanda via John there was also a change ... Meenu saw a lot of things were wrong when she came. She would say 'Who on earth could have done that? The right way to do it is this' ... In the review of 2005 there was rubbishing of what Meenu had done. In the review in Meenu's time it was the same. Amanda thought that what Meenu had done was not right.

This dismissal of predecessors' work, what this interviewee refers to as 'rubbishing', was facilitated by the centralisation of power in the position of the country director within ActionAid. This 'rubbishing' was mentioned frequently as contributing to the sudden shifts in approach referred to above, such as the moves to partnership and the human rights-based approach, and also as having a negative impact on institutional memory.[21] One former staff member commented:

New directors tend to delete what older ones have done. Amanda deleted what Meenu did. She didn't want to accept ... It comes back to institutional memory. Did Meenu take from Anthony? Subsequent people abandon process. Is this in development discourse for NGOs to discard the old? They have a big problem acknowledging. People don't want to acknowledge ... People insist on climbing a new ladder.

So, staff turnover and rubbishing of predecessors' initiatives enable trend-jumping, but what are the consequences of trend-jumping for initiatives such as ALPS? I highlight three here: initiatives being created without reference to the field level; insufficient attention to the implementation of initiatives; and a lack of attention paid to resolving difficult issues.

Creating initiatives disconnected from the field level

The first characteristic that I found of trend-jumping relates to a disconnection of policy-makers or creators of initiatives from the field level, which in turn can lead to over-idealism and over-ambition. It also leads to myths that idealise, but do not reflect, actual practice.

At international level, an example of this disconnection from the field level was noted by Newman (2011, p. 163) in relation to the 2008 paper which defined ActionAid's human rights-based approach for the first time:

> The paper was produced through discussions between senior international staff. Thus, this organisational understanding of rights and a rights-based approach was developed by those working at an abstract policy level, focused on international programming, and did not include staff engaged in local development work. The paper was offered as a way of sharing understanding of rights to staff across the organisation, but did not build from the reflections and experiences of programme staff.

The team which created ALPS was not much different, with only one team member out of six working at country level – the Gender Policy Analyst from Pakistan – and nobody from the sub-national level.[22] One former staff member who was part of the team spoke to me of the lack of focus on implementation at field level that he could only see in retrospect, noting, 'We didn't think through implementing reflection and review processes in many different [ActionAid] programmes, with power issues etc. ... We were quite naïve at the time. We expected local staff to figure this out, re. local power structures'.

Similarly, a staff member in Uganda commented that changes of approach are instituted at the national and international levels and 'at [these] higher levels people think things can move fast. The lower you go, the slower things go'. Thus, there is a risk that this disconnection from the field level leads to staff members at this level, who may not have the appropriate skills or much time, being left to implement new initiatives without sufficient guidance. This can mean that changes which have taken much internal reflection time at national or international levels do not have much impact on, or relevance to, the lives of intended beneficiaries. This is sometimes referred to as the danger of navel-gazing by organisations, which takes a lot of time but doesn't end up changing anything at operational level.

My interviews with community members in Uganda supported the notion that there was questionable relevance to intended beneficiaries of some of the changes which had taken place within ActionAid Uganda. Many of the community members with whom I spoke had collaborated with ActionAid since the late 1990s. Yet there was a striking lack of mention in my interviews with them of the myriad of changes that had occurred in ActionAid Uganda over the years. My questions about changes in the way that ActionAid worked invariably elicited responses about the types of inputs provided to the community, for instance that there were fewer cassava cuttings than before, that they now received goats instead of bicycles. The shift to partnership, the rights-based approach leading to more work with government and capacity building of communities to demand services, changes in participatory methodologies, new advocacy campaigns, and so on were not mentioned, except sometimes after considerable probing and, even then, usually only partnership was mentioned.

It would seem that this is either because the changes were not known about, or because they were not considered to be of sufficient importance to community members. Either way, these discussions support the contention that there had been a disconnect between organisational initiatives and field-level realities in ActionAid Uganda. One man in Katakwi, who had known ActionAid's work since they entered his community in the late 1990s, said simply, 'I have heard there have been changes in ActionAid Uganda and ActionAid International but there is no impact at this level'.

Insufficient attention to implementation

A second and related problem I found with changing approaches in ActionAid is that, despite the considerable profile and effort that often accompanied the introduction of new initiatives, there was insufficient time and effort put into ensuring that the approaches were then implemented properly. This imbalance was evident in my findings in general terms, as well as specifically in relation to ALPS.

The *Taking Stock 3* review team noted the tendency of ActionAid to set 'very ambitious' goals, strategies which were significant departures from the past, and a variety of associated themes and priorities, but then noted a tendency to 'flounder' as not enough attention was paid to implementation, including pilot testing, providing guidance to staff, and monitoring (Brown, 2010, p. 26). The example was given of the human rights-based approach:

> country visits found widespread confusion about what implementing the rights-based approach required in the field. AAI [ActionAid International] has now created an implementation manual for rights-based work on the ground—but it has not yet been published, nearly six years after the strategy was announced. The tools for program monitoring and evaluation are also only becoming available now. Systematically developing plans, pilot tests, manuals and monitoring and evaluation tools prior to adoption of new strategies could dramatically reduce 'flounder' time and enhance effective implementation. (ibid.)

Similarly, an interviewee in Uganda noted that for 'programme staff and indeed some other staff, ActionAid and ActionAid Uganda policies are hard to implement. The steps to implementation are not in place, often ideas have not been tested in practice and translating them into ways of working is very difficult'.

This lack of attention to implementation after introducing a new system was frequently noted in relation to ALPS. A former staff member, who had been part of the team which created ALPS, reflected to me that he had become conscious later that implementation is a science in its own right, and needs considerable effort and continuous reinforcement of messages; his view was that this was not done for ALPS. Another interviewee, a former staff member, noted, 'I think a major problem is that there has been an unwillingness to define ALPS practically, it has remained such an idealised theory that people (especially overloaded local workers who are poorly valued within the AA hierarchy) have struggled to know how to translate it into their practice'.

Similarly, at country level, academic Scott-Villiers (2002, p. 432), who was assisting with ALPS at an early stage, cited a staff member in Ethiopia who said after the launch of ALPS that staff 'never get time to review and evaluate any change we make, before a new one takes its place. Anyway it takes time to implement new procedures, it requires so many people to understand them and adjust. We have to hold workshops and pilots, all at the same time as fulfilling so many other plans'.

International staff members David and Mancini's (2004, p. 25) learning paper on ALPS concluded that the 'key lesson here is that putting the system in place is nowhere near enough to achieve real change'. Yet, considerable profile is often given to new initiatives such as ALPS before implementation has really begun, which can lead to the creation of myths.

ActionAid is not alone here. This imbalance of attention between the creation of initiatives and their implementation was noted by academic David Mosse (2005, p. 237) in a case study he conducted of a UK-funded rural development project in India over 12 years. He talked about this imbalance as a characteristic of managerialism which 'privileges policy over practice,' stating that, increasingly, 'international development is about generating consensus on approaches and framing models that link investment to outcomes, rather than implementation modalities (Quarles van Ufford et al, 2003:9) .... Questions of implementation are somebody else's problem'.

Mosse's description of how the project's model was widely presented and disseminated reminded me of the active dissemination of information about ALPS by staff members in the early 2000s, even before there was any practice to show, as I discussed earlier. He noted that, perhaps inevitably, 'managers of successful projects find an emphasis on dissemination more rewarding than struggling with the contradictions of implementation' (Mosse, 2005, p. 163).

The project that Mosse described widely disseminated its 'mythical' or idealised project model which 'establishes precisely the causal link between participatory processes and efficient implementation that is absent (or difficult to establish) in practice' (ibid., p. 162). A key characteristic of managerialist approaches, criticised by many authors in the development sector, is also relevant here: the tendency of these approaches to overstate the potential of technical solutions in development programming and hence understate significant dynamics in local contexts, particularly power dynamics that deeply challenge implementation. This brings me to the final problem with trend-jumping.

Lack of focus on resolving difficult issues

Coming back to ALPS and trend-jumping, adding to the disconnection from the field level, and the lack of attention to implementation, the third and final problem I found with frequently changing approaches was a lack of focus on resolving difficult issues which arise during implementation. My research found that some issues in ActionAid Uganda and ActionAid International came up continuously in reviews but never appeared to get resolved.

One example of this is how, in ActionAid Uganda, the issue of partner organisations at local level lacking constituencies and/or a commitment to poverty reduction, was often raised in documents over the 15-year period of my document review but was never resolved (ActionAid Uganda, 2005c). When the issue was raised, the subsequent action plan usually revolved around capacity building. Yet capacity building appears unlikely to be an appropriate solution for an organisation that is not representative or lacks commitment. Again, this seems to be overstating the potential of technical solutions. Some of ActionAid's partner organisations may simply have been the wrong partners and, from my interviews, it was clear that ActionAid staff members were acutely aware of this. Nevertheless, staff members had collaborated in capacity building programmes for partners over the years, in which they privately admitted they had no faith (of course, this also relates to the point on organisational hierarchy that I discussed above).

Examples at the international level relating to ALPS showed a similar tendency to side-step fundamental and structural issues hindering implementation. The ALPS review in 2004, as part of *Taking Stock 2*, made 21 recommendations to address the 'critical gaps' in ALPS (Guijt, 2004). However, the management response to the overall *Taking Stock 2* report did not appear to address these recommendations in any direct or substantive way.[23]

Subsequently, many of the issues identified in the 2004 review, such as those around power dynamics, organisational culture, and attitudes and behaviours, were present in the 2007 ALPS review and were still problematic at the time of my study. Yet, a new version of ALPS was created in 2011 with another new version planned for 2013, seemingly without grappling with the issues that kept being raised in reviews, such as power dynamics and staff attitudes and behaviours. It seems that the characteristic of discontinuity contributed to a focus on new versions of ALPS being created, without a serious focus on resolving the difficult issues of implementation in order to try to bring the practices closer to what was intended.

This leads to an impression that changes in approaches, new approaches, and generally trend-jumping can be, at least in part, a way to avoid dealing with difficult issues of implementation.

In my assessment, the continuous processes of change within ActionAid served to distract from the reality that the organisation was coming across fundamental blockages in some of its work that required serious structural shifts, which the organisation may not have been able or willing to make. ActionAid's responses to problematic issues tended to place a lot of faith in solutions in the future, usually assisted by new processes, guidelines, or approaches. In a book chapter on organisational breakdown and failure, Lewis (2017, p. 127) noted that people are 'keen to leave behind the failed expectations or disappointments of earlier periods so that they can engage with the "next big thing".'

The continuity of discontinuity

Thus, ALPS had been affected by each of these components of trend-jumping that I identified: the enabling factors of high staff turnover and the tendency of new staff to dismiss the work of predecessors. These then led to the consequences of the disconnection of new initiatives from the field level; the focus on creation of initiatives rather than their implementation; and the avoidance of difficult implementation issues. Collectively, these components led to trend-jumping, which constitutes a serious obstacle to the prospects of ALPS succeeding in enhancing ActionAid's accountability to intended beneficiaries.

Sogge (1996, pp. 16–17) summarises these issues in his discussion of the 'continuity of discontinuity' problem within the development NGO sector, asking why funding of NGOs is not more linked to outcomes:

> One reason is that agencies can just keep moving. Staff can often 'escape into the future' through a succession of short-gestation, photogenic projects and 'partners' … Moreover, aid fashions change, new staff arrive, a new crisis spot grips world

attention ... This 'continuity of discontinuity' afflicts not only private aid agencies of course, but it seems especially marked among them.

NGOs need to stay the course on localisation attempts and watch out for the tendencies described in this chapter in order to implement initiatives more effectively. They need to recognise how problematic high staff turnover is, and be alert to new staff who 'insist on climbing a new ladder' to make a name for themselves. They also need to design new initiatives (if indeed they are needed – reviewing current initiatives might be more productive), in close contact with the actual implementers at field level, with enough guidance and resources for implementation, and with regular reviews that actually tackle obstacles arising.

In the next chapter, I will introduce another major consideration for localisation attempts: the pressures on and interests of individual staff members.

CHAPTER TWELVE
Staff pressures and interests

There is very little discussion in the development literature about issues within the emotional realm of organisations such as the preferences and constraints of individual NGO workers. The impression that is given, often by default, is of NGO workers without their own agendas who automatically agree with and follow organisational strategies and whose personal lives never interfere with their work.

We all know that this is nonsense! Academics Norman Long and Dorothea Hilhorst have pushed back against this impression. Long (2001, p. 26) set out the 'actor-oriented approach' which rejected assumptions that development work can be understood only from its plans and its formal representations, and stressed the 'room for manoeuvre' of individual practitioners during implementation of programmes, as well as their distinctive histories, agendas, and biases. Hilhorst (2003, p. 24) used this approach in her detailed ethnography of an NGO in the Philippines, noting that staff 'bring their social networks and concerns to their NGO work', and these form part of powerful 'everyday discourses' which run alongside the official discourses, but which are invisible in NGO reports and public statements.

These descriptions very much resonated with my own work experiences and my findings from interacting with ActionAid Uganda staff and learning about their sources of stress. As well as pressures, I also encountered different interests of staff and partners which conflicted with the organisation's goals, for example instances of fraud involving staff and partner staff of ActionAid Uganda.

Lesson 7: Individual staff members' pressures and interests are highly relevant to localisation attempts and in some cases undermine them, and therefore must be recognised and understood.

In this chapter, I discuss both pressures and interests and how these negatively impacted on ActionAid's downward accountability.

Sources of stress and pressure

There is no question that significant events occurred in ActionAid Uganda during the period of my research, which created stress and pressure on staff.

In particular, livelihood concerns were a major consideration for ActionAid staff – not surprising in a developing country that has high unemployment rates and where staff members may have very limited job alternatives and their salaries may be supporting many extended family members. While not often recognised in the NGO literature, my research aligned with my own experience that livelihood concerns significantly shape staff members' perceptions of their work and hence shape their behaviour.

The issue of livelihood concerns helped to explain something I originally found very puzzling in my research. When Meenu Vadera became ActionAid Uganda country director in 1998, apart from the shift to partnership, the other major initiative Meenu started was an organisational development (OD) process. Very much in line with the discussion earlier about the importance of different types of staff when an international NGO wants to shift to localisation, the OD process aimed to turn ActionAid Uganda into a decentralised learning organisation. This required reflective and responsive staff members, rather than those who simply followed hierarchy.

Meenu hired veteran development thinkers Tina Wallace and Allan Kaplan as long-term consultants for this process. Wallace and Kaplan were to assist in reforming the organisational structure and ways of working of ActionAid Uganda to facilitate the new programme direction. The OD process consisted of regular workshops, leadership retreats, training, and various other activities with staff over the course of three years (Okwaare and Chapman, 2006). A group of about 40 members of the ActionAid Uganda leadership was included.

When I first began my exploratory research on ActionAid internationally, the Uganda country programme during Meenu's time stood out, from documents and international interviews, as a champion of ALPS as a result of this leadership. ActionAid Uganda seemed to be one of the few examples of country programmes that had seriously invested in organisational change for ALPS.

Authors praised the OD process as a rare example of investment in the necessary capacities for ALPS. The results of the 'intensive processes' in Uganda were said to have been 'transforming' (Chapman et al., 2003, p. 149; David and Mancini, 2004, p. 23; David et al., 2006, p. 147). Okwaare and Chapman (2006, p. 176) were complimentary, going so far as to say that the OD process in Uganda had 'encouraged greater participation, improved our analysis of power and gender, enhanced a culture of transparency and openness, and increased our accountability to poor people, partners and other stakeholders'.

This is where my puzzlement came in: I discovered during the early days of my field work that the perspective on the ground in Uganda was often very different, with mostly negative feedback on the OD process. I learnt over time that one of the main reasons for this negativity was the personal impact of the process on individuals. A few of the staff and former staff who were heavily involved in the OD process remembered it as a time of great personal growth and development, which was what I had heard from the international level. However, most interviewees in Uganda remembered the process primarily in terms of instability and job insecurity due to the restructuring taking place and the ensuing reduction in staff numbers when new partners were being taken on.

One typical quote from a former staff member is illustrative:

> The OD process caused anxiety. In any of this, people's individual job is at the core. These processes may affect organisations but in a deeper way they affect individuals and cause anxieties. People not knowing whether staying or going … What will we get from it? What will this cause? Work goes on but by people who are anxious … People didn't know what would happen and ended up leaving due to the insecurity.

This quote raises the harsh realities of livelihood concerns that can often be missed when organisations in developing countries are discussed in the abstract. These realities are all too dominant in the lives of many national and local staff, something I have witnessed throughout my working life. These kinds of staff issues help make up what Hilhorst terms *The Real World of NGOs* in her 2003 book.

Given that ActionAid Uganda was in a period of declining staff numbers at this time, with the significant increase in partnership, this insecurity is even more understandable.

Academic Scott-Villiers (2002, p. 434), who had worked with ActionAid, noted in an article on organisational change and the creation of ALPS, that:

> For many individuals, change is very risky, particularly for those at the bottom of a hierarchy. They may have spent years understanding the system and working out strategies for making the best of it. There are many frontline workers in ActionAid who worry a great deal about keeping their jobs, who are not in a position to change radically. Confident people, comfortable with power, will often be those to embrace change with most enthusiasm.

The objectives of the OD process around collective leadership and organisational learning could have been transformative for ActionAid's relationships with communities had they been achieved, but a failure to recognise the concerns of individual staff members was one factor which militated against this impact. A major manifestation of this was that the vast majority of Meenu's management team had left the organisation by 2004, including Meenu herself, which hindered the OD process having a lasting impact.

Another source of stress in ActionAid Uganda was excess workload, as I discussed earlier. This issue was palpable during my observations of daily life within the national office and within Local Rights Programme (LRP) offices. One staff member expressed common sentiments:

> The organisation knows about the overload but it's a 'Catch 22', it closes its eyes so it does not see it. Like someone is sick and the manager says, 'I'm so sorry you're sick and by the way, how about that report?' Things just get added. There is poor management, deafness and blindness to workload ... Families suffer.

> I am missing in the world in action. I'm active on Facebook to fill a gap to catch up with peers because I'm not there but I wish them happy birthday on Facebook and hope that they don't notice.

Excess workload was not a new issue in ActionAid Uganda and the stress that it caused was constantly mentioned in documentation.[24] At one point, sitting in a management team meeting in Kampala, I wrote in my notes, 'TIME, TIME, TIME, PRESSURE, PRESSURE, DEADLINES, DEADLINES'. Work-life balance received a score of only 26 per cent in the 2010 Staff Climate Survey in Uganda (Hewitt Associates, 2010). Similarly, at international level, internal management problems and work overload were a major theme in my interviews as causing stress to staff and leading to turnover.

In turn, these kinds of stresses and pressures have had a negative impact over the years on staff performance in terms of distraction from work and poor morale. They also increased turnover, which had impacts on the country programme in terms of loss of institutional memory and also relationships with external stakeholders. All of this will inevitably have an impact on the quality of the work of the country programme, including work relating to accountability to intended beneficiaries.

These stresses and pressures do not receive sufficient attention in the NGO literature, and yet clearly have profound effects on NGO work and the prospects of NGOs reaching their objectives.

Conflicting interests of staff

Apart from pressures on staff, a significant issue also arose in my research with respect to the interests of individual development practitioners, which can conflict with the organisation's aims of downward accountability. The example which emerged strongly was the instances of fraud by development practitioners in Uganda. I argue that fraud has two negative impacts on downward accountability prospects. First, it constitutes self-serving behaviour which is, of course, unlikely to bode well for accountability to intended beneficiaries. Second, it leads to the restrictive administrative procedures as noted earlier, which take the time of practitioners away from other work, such as community engagement.

Fraud was a major theme during my research, as I have referred to earlier. But interestingly, fraud and corruption in NGOs are not major themes in the NGO literature, even the accountability literature. When these issues are mentioned, it is usually in passing, as part of a larger list of problems with NGOs that result in the need for better accountability practices (see for instance Bendell, 2006; DENIVA, 2006; Brown, 2008). Fraud was also not a strong theme in my case study at ActionAid International level.

Yet my field work demonstrated that fraud was a feature of everyday life in ActionAid Uganda. My interviewees saw NGO fraud as a reflection of fraud and corruption in the wider society. One interviewee noted:

> You have to look at the history of the country, people have seen it all. They have no exposure to successful social movements. The focus is on the welfare of the family. So eating money is surviving.[25] There is no way to survive normally. If you are not corrupt as a government official, you will be seen as a non-performer, you won't be able to meet expectations of the community and your family.

As noted earlier, staff members and, even more frequently, partners were regularly being investigated for fraudulent practices in ActionAid Uganda. There was a zero-tolerance policy so even a small amount of money was taken seriously. There were a significant number of cases of staff and partner terminations as a result. Notably there were 613 audit queries being investigated in 2011, mostly related to partner organisations, although many of these may have ended up being due to low reporting capacity rather than fraud.

Nevertheless, during my field work, partnerships were suspended because of partner staff members misappropriating project inputs, including funds, for personal gain. This fraud took different forms. Sometimes, individuals had stolen organisational assets and absconded. For instance, in Katakwi, one partner staff member was reported to have taken a camera, a computer, the organisation's stamp, and a generator. In other instances, unauthorised payments were made with ActionAid funds which were seen to be for the personal gain of partner staff. A staff member was fired in one of the LRPs I visited for the misappropriation of small amounts of funds designated for programme activities (specifically money for tea).

In another LRP I visited, a previous LRP coordinator had been fired in recent years for infractions involving a conflict of interest in using a private business to provide services for the organisation (ActionAid Uganda, 2009a).

Several partners in the LRPs I visited were effectively suspended due to audit queries, which may or may not have turned out to be fraud. For instance, four out of the nine partners in one LRP were suspended at the time of my visit. Even though losses from fraud were reported to be minimal by interviewees working in finance, in part as ActionAid requires reimbursement of all losses by the partner organisation, all cases were taken seriously irrespective of the amount.

While it is not impossible that fraudulent practitioners can simultaneously promote a culture of downward accountability, it appears highly unlikely. This is the first reason why fraud is problematic for downward accountability.

The second reason is that, as a result of the perceived high risk of fraud, there was a very strong emphasis on internal audit within ActionAid Uganda.[26] Hence, as referred to earlier, strict and time-consuming administrative procedures were a central feature of the work of staff members, and this affected time available for other activities.

While I encountered fraud during my research with ActionAid and in the case study I discussed of a Concern partner in South Sudan, I should note that in the majority of my work with NGOs over the years, I did not encounter fraud. The point here is not that fraud is omni-present, but that it is present in some places and since it can clearly undermine localisation attempts, it's a factor that we should all take into account and not shy away from discussing. In my experience, there is often a reluctance by some stakeholders, particularly international NGO representatives, to frankly discuss fraud, and I don't find this helpful.

More broadly, we must recognise that people bring their stresses, pressures, and personal interests into their work lives and these will impact on localisation. Once again, an awareness of this possible obstacle is the first step to countering it. Supportive management structures can go a long way towards creating an open working environment and minimising the negative impacts that staff pressure and interests can have on programmes at community level.

In the next chapter, I look at international organisations' desire to retain control.

CHAPTER THIRTEEN
The retention of control

During my field work, I kept coming back to one fundamental question: to what extent does ActionAid really want to be accountable to its intended beneficiaries? This question is a bit heretical and may seem unfair, particularly because I selected ActionAid for my study precisely because they seemed to have made the most serious efforts to be downwardly accountable. So clearly on one level they did want to be accountable to communities.

But what struck me continuously in Uganda was that, even if ActionAid had well-implemented participation and transparency processes, with well-informed community members empowered to challenge the organisation, it would still appear to be unlikely that ActionAid would have (or perhaps would exercise) the flexibility to act, to any large degree, upon findings that clashed with what the organisation had already decided to do.

This is because it emerged strongly from my research in Uganda that ActionAid was firmly in control of decision-making on programme work, despite the shift to partnership and the commitments in ALPS that the priorities of community members would be central to decision-making. The organisation was not generally seen as flexible.

In this chapter, I make the case that ActionAid tightly controlled both partnerships and funded activities. I then look into why this was, and attribute ActionAid's need for control to three factors: restrictions of the current managerial system affecting NGOs; funding pressures linked to a desire for growth and to competition within the sector; and the simple fact that ActionAid had its own set of goals which may not have aligned with what community members may have requested. I also demonstrate that ActionAid's retention of control manifested itself in ways that were problematic for its downward accountability.

Lesson 8: The desire for retention of control by international organisations is real, even if it's sometimes unconscious. This should be borne in mind for localisation attempts as it may undermine them if it is not acknowledged and tackled by the organisation.

I found that, in Uganda, ActionAid dominated its partnership relationships at local level. This aligns with the findings of a study by Elbers and Schulpen (2011) on the partnerships of three international NGOs – ActionAid, Interchurch Organization for Development Cooperation, and Christian Aid – in three countries, Nicaragua, Ghana, and India. This study showed that ActionAid was the most intimately involved with its partners on project design and implementation and had the strictest rules. The study also showed that ActionAid tended to work with more dependent community-based partners, a point also noted by other authors and said to be particularly the case in Africa (ActionAid, 2010a; Imam, 2010).

This dominance was evident in ActionAid Uganda where there was very much a *parent-child* dynamic between ActionAid and partners. Interestingly, this language was used by many partners themselves to describe the relationship (and incidentally those partners were not saying this as a negative). The external evaluation of ActionAid Uganda in 2011 referred to the ActionAid-partner relationship as 'headmaster-pupil' (Kithinji et al., 2010, p. 70). Partners I interviewed generally noted that they had good opportunities to provide feedback to ActionAid, for instance through partner Participatory Review and Reflection Processes (PRRPs), but that this did not usually lead to change. This was corroborated by staff. One staff member noted:

> Partners used to be shy but then they would point out what is wrong … Then discussion was a strong learning tool, but to what extent did ActionAid accept feedback? … ActionAid needed mechanisms to react and respond. It became a formality over time, to document it etc. But what about implementation? How many people were held responsible? Was there any discipline? It became routine. If you read the PRRP reports you will see the same issues in each report.

One example of this was the issue of late disbursement of funds by ActionAid to partners, which was mentioned in almost every

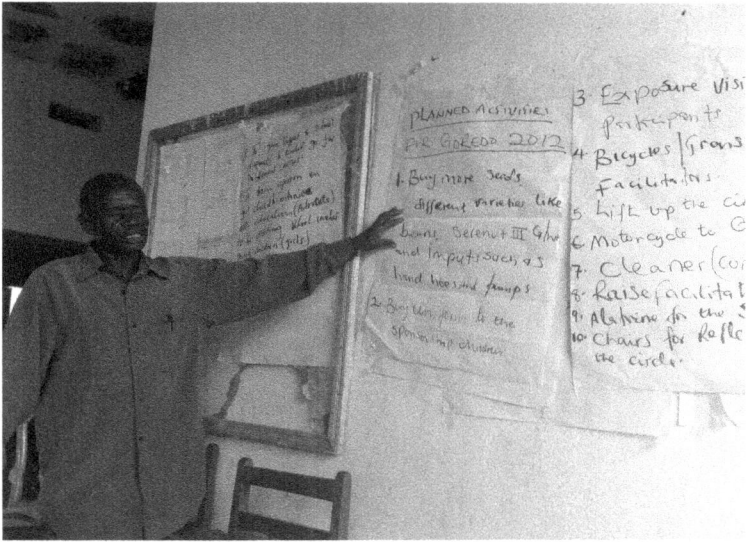

Photo 13.1 Presentation at PRRP in Gogonyo, Pallisa LRP, 25 July 2011

interview I conducted with partners as the main problem in their relationship. Documents show that this issue had been constantly raised by partners over the years, but that ActionAid had not resolved it despite the continuous feedback (KASDA, 2005; ActionAid Uganda, 2007; Toroma Partnership Project, 2011).

In addition to its strongly influential role with respect to partners, my research illustrated that ActionAid Uganda also exerted a significant degree of control over the activities which were carried out at community level. In five of the six PRRPs I attended, community members were asked to give a wish list of desired activities. This can be seen in a photograph of one partner in Gogonyo where the list includes purchase of seeds, uniforms for sponsored children, increased stipends for facilitators, chairs for activities, a salary for a cleaner, and a latrine for visitors (Photo 13.1).

However, in none of these PRRPs did ActionAid or the partner give any conclusive feedback to these requests or plans, nor was there any prioritisation done with community members. In each case, the flipcharts from the PRRPs were taken away by ActionAid or the partner. Furthermore, it was clear from partner interviewees that ActionAid always had the final say on the budget and how it should be allocated in its review process of partners' proposals.

So, ActionAid was in control. This theme also arose at international level. Two former staff members and a consultant, Rosalind David, Antonella Mancini, and Irene Guijt (2006, p. 141) noted that 'much of the difficulties [*sic*] that ActionAid experienced in translating ALPS into reality was to do with control over resources and activities – not wanting to let go of control, and fear of what would happen if we did'. As I thought about why ActionAid needed this level of control, this quote made me wonder whether there was a link between control over resources and over activities. Was ActionAid generally seen as controlling because it was trying to retain control over its funding resources?

The link between control and funding sources

Some partners interviewed felt that one reflection of ActionAid's controlling engagement in its partnerships was the fact that, despite working with partners at Local Rights Programme (LRP) level, ActionAid still maintained its own offices at that level. In fact, there had been attempts in ActionAid Uganda in previous years to have partners manage the sponsorship process directly, thus potentially untying ActionAid from being based at local level. However, initial attempts were not successful as partners failed to fulfil sponsorship requirements adequately, thus jeopardising the continuation of sponsors' commitments. The 2005 evaluation recommended that: 'Given that it is AAIU's [ActionAid International Uganda's] cash cow, a change process should be developed to regain control of sponsorship management by AAIU staff rather than through partners and individuals not employed by AAIU' (Kabenge et al., 2005, p. 43).

ActionAid implemented this recommendation and at the time of my research, with the exception of one partner, sponsorship was managed by ActionAid. This development suggested that a major reason for ActionAid Uganda's perceived need to retain control over partners and programming at the local level was its sponsorship funding. Keeping sponsors, sponsored children, and their parents happy to maintain the flow of letters, photographs, and money was a key concern for ActionAid, as the high prioritisation of meeting sponsorship requirements in the country programme illustrated.

But did the need to manage the sponsorship process mean that ActionAid had to control activities? I found that while sponsorship funding created incentives for ActionAid to keep control over reporting (including photos, case studies, and child letters), it did not actually restrict the type of work that was done or how it was done. In fact, sponsorship funding left considerable scope for ActionAid to make decisions on programming, as was noted in interviews and in meetings I attended in Uganda. As Newman (2011, p. 121) noted:

> The organisational management systems emerged to ensure that ActionAid would 'give account' to the individual sponsor, based on the deliverables agreed when contracts were signed. But the sponsors had minimal expectations of holding ActionAid to account. This gave the organisation great flexibility to be experimental or dramatically change direction; and many people whom I interviewed noted that it was this broad and dispersed funding base that enabled ActionAid to embrace the rights-based approach to such an extent.

And yet, ActionAid was considered relatively inflexible and controlling. Thus, the fact that ActionAid received sponsorship funding does not explain why it retained so much control over the type of work which is done. A second possible explanation for ActionAid's retention of control was its institutional donor funding.

Institutional donors and managerialism

A common theme in the NGO literature at the time of my research was that institutional donors (i.e. not individuals) were increasingly requesting results to be predicted in advance and creating incentives for NGOs to keep control over programming, rather than handing this over to local partners or communities. This was linked to the trend towards managerialism that I spoke about earlier. Authors noted that the desire to maintain and retain control is central to the assumptions of managerialism and the related trend of New Public Management[27] (Harding, 2013). Wallace and Chapman (2004, p. 25) cited the argument of moral philosopher Alasdair MacIntyre that 'it is a modern bureaucratic managerial illusion that people or organisations have the ability to control and shape events. Yet the belief lies at the heart of the new public management'.

This need of organisations for control influences who else can feed into decisions. Mosse (2005, p. 161), discussing the acclaim the UK Government-funded rural development project in India received for its participatory processes, noted that, despite appearances, the 'delivery of these programmes was, however, far too important to be left to participatory (i.e. farmer-managed) processes; hence the strong vertical control of activities and implementation'.

Indeed, the NGO literature suggested that organisations which were using a results-based management approach tended to have strong incentives for control and for predictable outcomes, despite perhaps claiming in their communications that they were working in a participatory manner. Academic Patrick Kilby (2004a, p. 218), in his study of 15 Indian NGOs implementing empowerment programmes, spoke of the same issue of NGOs being reluctant to cede control:

> The findings also point to fundamental limitations of develop-
> ment agencies as empowerment agents … Joshi and Moore, for
> example, are 'skeptical of the capacity or willingness of any but
> the most exceptional organizations to encourage or even toler-
> ate the autonomous and potentially antagonistic mobilization
> of their own client groups' (2000, p. 49). Skepticism is likely
> to be even more warranted if a development agency such as a
> contractor has a formal contractual relationship with a donor
> who has prescribed the expected outcomes and approaches to
> be taken in managing these development programs, something
> often required in results-based frameworks.

As Kilby (2004a, p. 209) further noted, 'The core problem remains – the application of results-based management to the management of development projects leaves little space for a role of the beneficiary in project design, planning, or even implementation'.

Thus, a strong case can be made that trends of institutional donors towards managerialism and results-based management will not be conducive to real downward accountability. But given that ActionAid has traditionally been largely child sponsorship-funded, it would not have been thought to be as vulnerable to the demands of results-based management as some of its peers.

However, ActionAid's dependence on institutional donors had increased since 2002 and, moreover, it was actively seeking more institutional funding during the period of my research. Official donors such as the UK's Department for International Development (DfID) and the Danish International Development Agency comprised 31 per cent of global income in 2011, compared with 48 per cent from child sponsorship (ActionAid, 2012). The proportion of institutional donor funding in Uganda was even higher in 2011 at 45 per cent (ActionAid Uganda, 2012b).

In addition, it appeared that ActionAid was quite influenced by the managerialist tendencies within the sector even if it shouldn't have been so directly affected by the related funding pressures.[28] ActionAid interviewees at the international level were critical of the organisation's acceptance of results-based management demands of donors, particularly DfID, noting that ActionAid had resisted these requirements when they were first introduced in around 2000 (Eyben, 2006). Wallace and Chapman (2004, p. 27), in their study of policies and procedures of aid disbursement from the UK to Uganda and South Africa, which included ActionAid, observed that:

> It had initially been thought that agencies with significant amounts of untied funding (from the public for example) would be freer to shape their own systems and procedures. However, it became clear, during the first phase of the research, that they were heavily influenced by the new public management agenda through their trustees, and sometimes their [Chief Executive Officers] formerly of the business sector. They were also influenced by their close relations with key donors.

It would also seem likely, given the movement of staff within the sector and other interactions, that some 'institutional isomorphism' takes place whereby ActionAid comes to resemble its peers, some of which are under more severe managerial pressures (DiMaggio and Powell, 1983). This relates to a point made by a senior staff member in Uganda, after the initial presentation of my findings, that institutional donors may be affecting NGOs such as ActionAid indirectly, by having a dominant influence on the NGO sector as a whole and how it operates. Similarly, in a conference presentation on ALPS, staff members David and Mancini (2003, p. 7) cautioned that 'ActionAid needs to boldly challenge its own internal tendency to apply management-centred "logical" and "linear" thinking, as well as that imposed from outside'.

Thus, it seems as though the influence of institutional donors and managerialism formed at least part of the explanation for why ActionAid might have been keen on control. Analysing this a bit more deeply, I found that competition and growth within the sector was also key here.

Funding pressures from competition and growth

I found resource dependency theory helpful in trying to understand why ActionAid might have felt pressure to retain control over programming and fit into institutional donor strictures, despite not seeming overly dependent on such funds. According to this theory, organisations make decisions based on institutional survival and growth concerns (Pfeffer and Salancik, 1978). An African proverb, quoted by Kramer (1981, p. 158) graphically illustrates this point: 'If you have your hand in another man's pocket, you must move when he moves'.

Given that ActionAid was widely viewed by my interviewees to have a relatively stable, long-term sponsorship base, the issue of institutional survival did not seem to be a major concern. However, the desire for organisational growth and, related to this, competition in the NGO sector, was something that came up frequently. There is much evidence in the broader literature that it is not only the fight for survival that ties NGOs into funding relationships; they also fight for growth (Edwards and Hulme, 1996; Wallace and Porter, 2013).

Growth, linked to the goals of greater influence and impact, was a major ambition for ActionAid (Jayawickrama and Ebrahim, 2013). David and Mancini (2011, p. 246), in a discussion on the negative impact of the results-based management culture on the kind of changes attempted by ALPS, noted: 'The big elephant in the room is the imperative for institutional growth, with large [international] NGOs driven to work in more countries and sectors'.

Some staff members expressed that the organisation's desire for growth had negative implications for ALPS implementation in particular. One staff member stated, 'We cannot fully reach ALPS purposes within the current dynamics of the organisation. Actually, if there is a problem, I think it is not in ALPS per se but in our current programmatic ambition and sometimes, dispersion'. Kilby's (2004a, p. 218) study, similarly, noted the reluctance of some NGOs in India to be accountable to beneficiaries because of their desire for growth: 'These NGOs felt that direct accountability mechanisms to the constituency might in some ways compromise them institutionally, and limit their capacity for expansion or dealing with other stakeholders such as donors'.

Related to the desire for growth, another key factor influencing the funding pressure ActionAid felt was competition with peer NGOs. ActionAid's 2011 Financial Report spoke of 'increased competition for reducing development aid budgets' (Lynch-Bell, 2012, p. 13). Many other documents speak of the pressure ActionAid felt from increased competition within the sector, particularly in the context of the economic recession at that time in Western Europe, and how this led to the need to maintain a certain profile (Bertin, 2004; ActionAid, 2010c). Authors outside ActionAid also pointed to the increasingly corporate and competitive fundraising culture which called for evidence of an international NGO's distinctiveness and value-added.

NGOs' own priorities

I found one final factor affecting why NGOs such as ActionAid did not appear to be flexible to community priorities: simply that the organisation had other competing priorities that were more important to it at a given point in time. This brings in the notion from the actor-oriented approach, that NGOs have room for manoeuvre, a point which is not often focused on in the NGO accountability literature that tends to focus more on impacts of donor pressures on NGOs. The literature, at times, appears to blame donors, as though NGOs were bound to accept any funding under any conditions that a donor might impose, in order to ensure survival and growth.

Given this room for manoeuvre, NGOs may have a host of objectives and priorities to which they are committed, which may not align with what community members may request at any point in time. As Obrecht (2011) noted simply, NGOs are set up with their own sets of goals. ActionAid, for instance, has many priorities, strategies, and themes at international and national levels, feeding into major ambitions to which the organisation wants to contribute.

For example, ActionAid's strategic plan for 2012–17 set out five 'mission objectives' including ten 'key change promises', and seven organisational objectives, along with the organisation's vision, mission, and theory of change (ActionAid, 2011a). Community priorities, whatever they might be, are by nature unpredictable, which interferes with NGO internal planning and fundraising methodologies. In addition, in some instances, specific community priorities can be problematic for NGOs. This was the case in ActionAid Uganda during my period of study when the organisation's strategy was heavily centred on the rights-based approach, which focused a lot on government's responsibility to provide services, whereas community members almost invariably requested the provision of inputs directly from NGOs.[29]

In sum, my research suggested that ActionAid's prioritisation of obtaining and retaining control, vis-à-vis communities and partners, militated against downward accountability and was likely to be caused by a combination of funding dynamics, sectoral managerialist pressures, and the desire of ActionAid to fulfil other goals. These are quite deep issues which don't have quick fixes, but recognition of and internal reflection on them will help to reduce their negative potential impacts on localisation.

In the next chapter, I will look at the role of perceptions and optics in shaping NGO behaviour.

CHAPTER FOURTEEN
The power of optics

The reason I approached ActionAid in the first place was that I had heard so many positive things about their Accountability, Learning and Planning System (ALPS) in general, including in Uganda. But the reality I found on the ground was very different. As I have discussed throughout this book, there were formidable obstacles both at operational and at a more fundamental, structural level to ActionAid being more accountable to its intended beneficiaries. Many ActionAid staff were well aware of this and spoke frankly with me about the weaknesses in the organisation's downward accountability practice, albeit often only when they knew I had already seen these weaknesses myself.

Yet, the positive framing of ALPS continued, frequently from the same people!

I coined the phrase *brochure talk* during my field work, to describe times, particularly at the beginning of interviews, when staff or former staff automatically began to give me public relations-type descriptions of their work, as might be read in a brochure. This would be the official line about ALPS, presenting an image of how things should be, rather than how they actually are.

To what extent this was conscious or subconscious in individual cases was hard to say. In general, I felt that the brochure talker was aware that what they said did not reflect a reality which they had themselves observed. In many cases I was able to prove this; I would work at the beginning of interviews to communicate to the interviewee that I knew there were challenges to working in the sector and that this interview was a safe space for being critical. In other words, I would let the interviewee know that I was a practitioner in the sector myself, not only a researcher of it (and if applicable, I would mention having been at Participatory Review and Reflection Process (PRRP) sessions, etc.). Often this would lead quickly to a change in tone and content of an interview, away from the generic, positive talking points. In one case, after an interview with a former staff member had started with him giving some of the common idealist descriptions of ALPS, and after I had subsequently alluded to the difficulties that I knew usually exist given my own work with NGOs in the region, the interviewee stopped and said, 'Oh. I didn't realise you knew that stuff'. He then proceeded to give me a much more critical perspective!

The important feature of brochure talk is that it is designed to present a positive image, regardless of what the realities might be. I noted that ActionAid Uganda staff members, while exceptionally self-critical at times, were generally skilled in brochure talk. One of my international interviewees spoke of the tendency for ActionAid staff to 'learn the language and rattle away'. Another former staff member of ActionAid Uganda described ActionAid as 'seduced by language and rhetoric'.

Language in Aidland

To provide more context for the discussion of brochure talk and optics, it is worth taking a moment to look at critiques of how language is used in the development sector, in ways which can often be opaque, exclusive, and misleading. Anthropologist Raymond Apthorpe's description of 'Aidland', in a scathing critique of the aid sector, is illustrative here:

> the Aidland balloon has come to have a very thick skin. Among other things this allows it to contain securely a lot of very hot air that is produced by relentless use of vogue keywords – 'participation', 'partnership', 'empowerment', 'civil society', 'democracy' and the like as well as the innocuous little 'local ownership'. Pumped-up to a very high density, this opacity acts to keep ordinary words and language usages out, ordinary sense-making too (Apthorpe, 'Alice in Aidland', 2016, p. 16, unpublished).

Other authors similarly commented on the way in which language in the development sector tends to be vague and unclear, and also how this lack of clarity facilitates the continuation of the status quo. Mosse (2005, p. 230), in the aforementioned case study of a rural development project in India, remarked that, 'Policy discourse generates mobilising metaphors ("participation", "partnership", "governance") whose vagueness, ambiguity, and lack of conceptual precision is required to conceal ideological differences'.

Scott-Smith (2013, p. 107), speaking of his experience as an NGO worker in Malawi caught up in the managerialist framework, talked of the obscurity of 'development speak': 'these assumptions – that everyone agrees on the basic concepts, that everyone supports the aims of the project, that our overall objectives are good – tend to disguise the contested nature of our work, and obscure how often we become separated from the way people speak, think, talk, and desire at the local level'.

Similarly, Cornwall and Brock (2005, p. 1), in an article on the power of development 'buzzwords', spoke of the 'consensus narrative' in the development sector. The authors also pointed to external legitimacy benefits of such a narrative, noting that the 'fine-sounding words that are used in development policies do more than provide a sense of direction: they lend the legitimacy that development actors need in order to justify their interventions' (ibid.).

Brochure talk is usually replete with jargon and it is rhetorical in that it is designed to persuade the audience or reader that the ideal is actually real.[30] An example of this kind of use of language was provided by Watkins et al. (2012) in an article on the sociology of development NGOs. The authors quoted from a case study of NGOs and farmers' associations in Guinea-Bissau which clearly illustrated rhetoric or brochure talk targeted to a particular external audience. Some of the farmers, 'usually among the most charismatic and eloquent' were chosen:

> by their capacity to accept and reproduce the development 'cargo-cult' rhetoric of the NGOs toward foreigners, be they evaluators, researchers or simple visitors: 'we are poor but we work hard' (anós i pobre, má nô pega teso). The other farmers called them the project 'bards' (djidios) ... They also appeared to be the ones most willing to mouth donor agendas in order to gain access to the material and symbolic resources that donors provided (Temudo, 2005 cited in Watkins et al., 2012, p. 261).

Therefore, in various ways, by being vague, obscure or rhetorical, the way language is used in the development sector facilitates brochure talk.

Transparency boards

One of the most striking examples of brochure talk that I found involved transparency boards, another key process of ALPS. Transparency boards were one of the most widely cited features of ALPS, along with PRRPs. The ALPS guidelines stated that 'Alps encourages open information through bulletin boards and posters easily accessible to communities with details of our own plans and budgets' (ActionAid, 2006a, p. 8). I will give two examples here of where I observed brochure talk in relation to transparency boards in Kenya and Uganda.

Transparency boards in Kenya

At the time of my research, the most celebrated example of transparency boards in practice was in ActionAid Kenya. A case study on these transparency boards was presented at the internal ActionAid workshop on ALPS and accountability which I attended in 2010.

In principle, transparency boards in Kenya displayed detail on the expenditure of ActionAid and partners, in order that members of the communities could study this information and ask questions or make suggestions on expenditure (ActionAid Kenya, 2006). However, when the case study of transparency boards was presented at this workshop, serious shortcomings were highlighted by the ActionAid Kenya staff members:

> In terms of understandability of the transparency boards and its content, however, various gaps were realized. First, Partners and Rights Holders felt that the financial details provided on these boards are too general … for the partners to understand such critical information as; who/which Community Based Organization (CBO) has received resources from [ActionAid Kenya], an aspect that would help in tracking their use … Further still, the fact that the decision on what to put on the Transparency Board is usually a prerogative of [ActionAid Kenya's LRP] staff limits the simplicity of the information posted on these boards, thus hindering participation of the Rights Holders in auditing the use of the funds. (ActionAid Kenya, 2010, p. 19)

The absence of critical and simple information would appear to be a serious shortcoming with respect to transparency boards.

An analysis of photographs from the case study presentation by ActionAid Kenya is illustrative. The photographs show two different types of transparency board The first, Photo 14.1, was an ActionAid board (ActionAid Usigu) which listed the sectors supported, for instance 'women's rights'; the broad objectives of this support, for instance 'increased number of women accessing rights, participation in governance'; and the anticipated amount of funds available. The ActionAid board also detailed expenditure from the previous year by sector, for instance 'cross-cutting issues'; what the funds were spent on, for instance the Ministry of Health's tuberculosis programme; and the total amount per sector. The transparency board was entirely in English and not very reader-friendly, with small text. In terms of the information provided, it certainly gave some insights into the ActionAid programme but, as mentioned in the case study presentation, the board lacked important information about partners and activities, which was key information for community members.

The second example, Photo 14.2, from a local partner called Barokwiri Abidha Magombe Achuodho, was clearer, though information was limited and in English. The board mentioned how much money was spent, from which donor, which activities were done, and the extent to which they were completed.

Therefore, this case study illuminated both positive and negative features of transparency boards. On the one hand, transparency boards were still in existence in ActionAid Kenya a number of years after the launch of ALPS. In addition, partners had clearly been influenced by ActionAid to have their own boards – the same case study speaks of local government offices who had also begun the practice. This was very positive.

However, while the boards provided some relevant programme information, the case study paper and photos did not suggest that intended beneficiaries were able to obtain basic programme information with the level of accessibility that was intended. All boards were in English, and the ActionAid board, in particular, was quite difficult to read and contained limited information.

Another key issue raised in the case study presentation from Kenya was the ability or willingness of community members to question ActionAid, similar to the point raised regarding the Nepal social audits earlier: 'According to the rights holders, their lack of access to information on the resources provided to their organizations

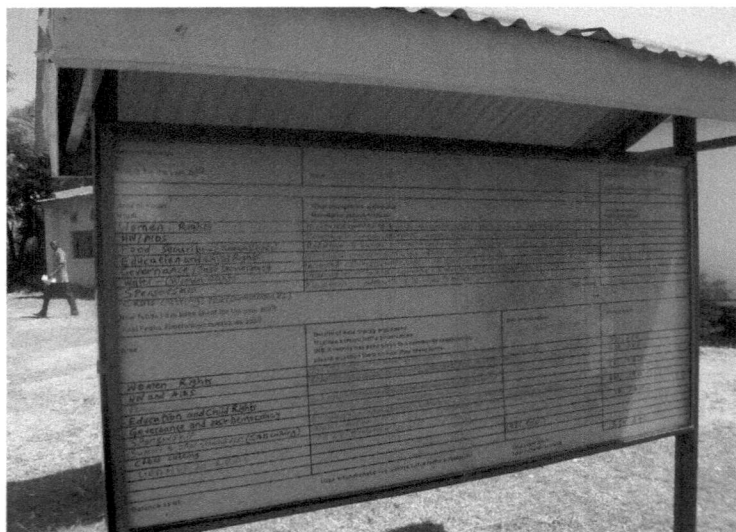

Photo 14.1 ActionAid Usigu Transparency Board
Source: Ireri, 2010, p.18

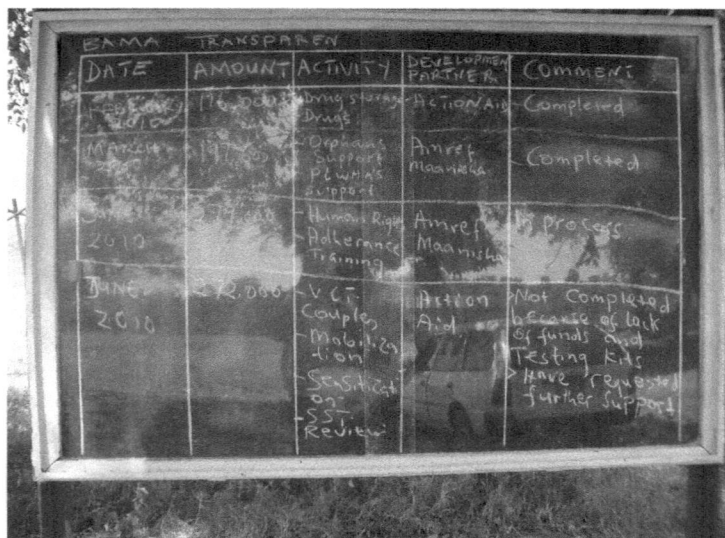

Photo 14.2 Barokwiri Abidha Magombe Achuodho Transparency Board
Source: Ireri, 2010, p. 21

coupled with the fear of [ActionAid Kenya's] withdrawal of its support from the area in case of rights holders' question prevented them from raising any issues with the organization' (ActionAid Kenya, 2010, p. 22).

This resonates with a quote from a partner in Kenya in David et al.'s paper (2006, p. 146). Partners were asked to make honest criticisms of ActionAid during a participatory process and one partner responded saying, 'We can only respond to the questions raised if you can promise that you will not victimize us by cancelling our project'.

Interestingly, despite the shortcomings of the transparency boards and the lack of critical engagement, as acknowledged in the Kenya case study paper, I was struck by how the tone of the paper was nevertheless upbeat. The paper listed impacts which included 'Impact One: Transparent Boards have ensured that [ActionAid Kenya] remains accountable to all the stakeholders at all levels, particularly the rights holders' (ActionAid Kenya, 2010, p. 17). Given the paper's own findings, this appeared to be a considerable overstatement and an example of brochure talk that suggested a need to portray ActionAid and ALPS in a positive way, while also acknowledging a different reality, in detail, in the very same paper.

Transparency boards in Uganda

I had a similar experience in Uganda when I sought out transparency boards at local level, in that the boards were present in some cases, but not always doing what they were supposed to be doing.

One particular example stood out. In Masindi, when I asked a partner about transparency boards, the staff searched through a bunch of used flipchart papers within their office and showed me one with budget figures from the first half of 2010 (this was in April 2011) which they said constituted their 'transparency board' (Photo 14.3).

It was extraordinary that, while these flipcharts contained old information and were not remotely transparent to outsiders given the way they were stored, the partner was familiar with the terminology and produced something called a 'transparency board' on demand. This suggested a tick-box approach to the process, very much concerned with perceptions or *optics*.[31]

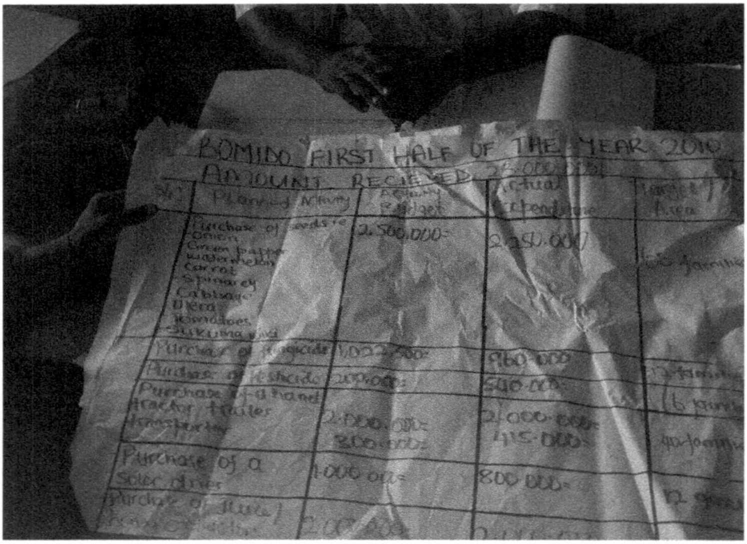

Photo 14.3 Partner Transparency Board in Masindi Local Rights Programme (LRP), April 2011.

Therefore, brochure talk, when it did not appear to match with realities, helped to build and maintain a myth of ALPS, both inside and outside the organisation, as being strong on the achievement of downward accountability. It did this by projecting a positive image, regardless of actual practice. In the remainder of this chapter I ask, what was the incentive for staff to maintain this myth?

Optics and managerialism

To try to understand this tendency of ActionAid staff to use brochure talk, my supervisor David suggested that I look up the literature on *disjuncture*, meaning the disconnection between what NGOs portray and what they actually do.

I found useful studies looking at accountability mechanisms that didn't work in practice, but were still used even though people knew this. For example, I found research by Wallace et al. (2007) who conducted case studies of UK-funded NGOs in Uganda and South Africa which were using a results-based management framework. The authors took the example of the logical framework (logframe), supposedly a key accountability tool to be used throughout the lifecycle of a programme – and a tool that most practitioners in the sector know well.[32] The authors found that, while NGOs made enormous efforts to craft the logframe to the format accepted by the donor, the tool was only being used at the planning and proposal stage: 'All said the tools do not work once implementation starts. There were no exceptions; this is a really striking finding' (ibid., p. 165).

Similarly, Roberts et al. (2005, p. 1851) studied the impact of accountability mechanisms of a 'distinctly northern type' on NGOs in Oaxaca, Mexico. They found that NGOs in Oaxaca resisted burdensome demands by developing certain practices, such as having one set of financial books for donors and another which reflected how money was actually used.

Finally, in a case study from Tanzania, Goddard and Assad (2006) discovered that NGOs were paying three times the normal rate to hire international audit firms mainly to enhance their image with donors, with no history of actually implementing any recommendations which might ensue from these audits.

These examples reminded me of Hilhorst's case study in the Philippines that I mentioned earlier, and the divide she saw between what actually happened within the NGO and what was reported in accounts. They also reminded me of Mosse's case study in India and of the co-existence of different worlds within the same project that he described: the official world of policies, proposals, and reports which are relayed to donors and other stakeholders, and the world of practice, or what actually happens.

What these examples have in common is that they are prioritising perceptions and optics, over real-world utility. They are also responding to the demands of managerialism and its manifestation of results-based management (Kilby, 2004b; Wallace et al., 2007; Shutt, 2009).

As I discussed earlier, managerial approaches tend to overstate the potential of technical solutions in development programming and hence understate contextual dynamics, particularly power dynamics. Within this 'technical-rational' realm, it is assumed that implementers of development work have control over what is needed to produce the 'results', which are therefore predictable (Harding, 2013, p. 131). Chris Mowles (2013, pp. 51–52), in an article criticising managerial methods of planning and evaluation, noted that 'International development is no exception for the use of abstract and logical methods for regulating social life ... There has been a proliferation of abstract tools and techniques of management, based on assumptions of predictability and control'.

But why do NGOs continue to go along with managerialist donor approaches, even in cases such as those mentioned above in Mexico, South Africa, Uganda, and Tanzania when the requirements were irrelevant to actual practice? This is the same question I asked earlier in this chapter about ActionAid practitioners: why do they use brochure talk about ALPS initiatives which they know, on some level, to be untrue?

From my research and my experience, I contend that there are two main needs of NGOs fulfilled by the prioritisation of optics and the continuation of the disjuncture between rhetoric and reality: external legitimacy and internal legitimacy.[33]

External legitimacy

An important part of the reason why the disjuncture persists between what is reported and what is done in development NGOs is the need to be legitimate to external stakeholders, particularly donors, in the context of NGOs' resource dependence. This includes satisfying the managerial requirements of donors in the short-term and also enhancing and safeguarding the NGO's reputation in the long term.

In the study I mentioned above of Tanzanian NGOs, Goddard and Assad (2006, p. 394) found that the accounting practices adopted by the organisations, which they associated with 'creeping managerialism', mainly served the needs of external stakeholders: 'the primary purpose of accounting was its symbolic use in navigating legitimacy. This transcended any technical or even informational contributions of accounting reports. It also transcended the use of internal accounting information within the organisations for decision-making' (ibid., p. 377).

As I discussed earlier, resource dependency theory helps to explain why NGOs are so motivated by external legitimacy, even when it means going along with practices which don't serve their purported purpose. The pressures of survival, growth, and competition are real. And of course, it is often genuinely believed by practitioners that doing what is needed for resource mobilisation is for a good cause.

In an article on the 'insulation' of development workers, Scott-Smith (2013, p. 108) reflected on his experience as an NGO practitioner in Malawi saying, 'We were always willing to bend our aims and objectives to the demands of donors, because the mantra was growth: more income, more impact, more results'.

It is clear from the literature that many development NGOs are dependent on major bodies such as governments for their funding in an increasingly competitive fundraising environment (Harris, 2011; Baur and Schmitz, 2012). Therefore, playing along with donors' managerial requirements, no matter how seemingly irrelevant to their day-to-day work, is a rational decision.

So resource dependence and the desire for external legitimacy provide one explanation for why NGOs play along with managerialist practices which do not appear to work in terms of managing programmes.

In ActionAid's case, its reputation for being accountable to intended beneficiaries, a reputation, by all accounts, significantly strengthened by the public relations coup of ALPS, presumably helped it to raise funds from sponsors and institutional donors in the context of competition within the sector. Apart from the many publications by external authors mentioning ALPS, bilateral and multilateral donors, peer NGOs, and networks had frequently requested presentations on ALPS at various conferences (David and Mancini, 2004, p. 17). Examples included the Organisation for Economic Co-operation and Development (OECD) Evaluation group, the Berlin Civil Society Centre, and the British Overseas NGOs for Development (BOND) network.

ActionAid focused on its closeness to communities within its fundraising literature. For instance, the following statement from the organisation's website was illustrative: 'We're not about giving handouts or telling people what to do, because in the long run we know that doesn't work. Instead, we use our resources, influence and experience to help people find their own solutions. We listen to what people really want and need' (ActionAid, 2013).

Along the same lines, the logical framework designed by ActionAid in 2009 to receive Partnership Programme Arrangement funding from the UK's Department for International Development (DfID) states under the heading 'Niche' that, 'Action Aid's rights based approach is based on the primacy of rights holders as the key actors of change, claiming rights for themselves ... This has also

led to our particularly strong emphasis on accountability to poor
and excluded people – both pushing for this in the aid sector and
holding ourselves to account' (ActionAid, 2009, p. 1).

This increased legitimacy likely contributed positively to
fundraising. This is not unique to ActionAid. In his case study in
India, Mosse (2005, p. 162) pointed out that, 'Participatory
models and ideals of self-reliance are often more part of the way
projects work as systems of representations, oriented upwards and
outwards to wider policy goals and institutions that secure reputation
and funding … than part of their operational systems'. This helps
to explain why the ongoing disjuncture between the theory and
practice exists, since NGOs benefit from the representation of their
accountability practices matching with their theory, even if this
does not reflect reality, as in the case of ALPS.

I think many of us in the development sector would have an
intuitive sense of this external legitimacy dimension being an
incentive for optics. But I will argue that there is more: a lesser-
known internal legitimacy aspect playing a role.

Internal legitimacy

The development NGO literature has a tendency to attribute the
causality for many NGO decisions to donors, particularly in the context
of increasing managerialism. I argue that legitimacy in the eyes of its
internal stakeholders is also an important part of the explanation for
why NGOs prioritise optics and why they continue to use and talk
up accountability mechanisms, even though they know that the
mechanisms in question are not working as intended.

An example of the benefits to internal stakeholders of sustaining
the disjuncture between policy and practice can be found in an
account given by Hilhorst (2003) of her ethnographic research in
the Philippines. The author described a model for creating self-
reliant 'people's organisations' that the NGOs in her case study
used. This was a 'step-by-step' model that 'leans on notions of
modern organizations and the linearity of planned intervention'
(ibid., p. 103). Hilhorst came across a paradox:

> The contrast between the intimate knowledge of actual village
> organizing processes and the idealistic or normative way in
> which NGO actors talked about the step-by-step organizing

model amazed me. At some point I had the idea that the model only had a formal life. In meetings of the NGOs it was used to report on organizing processes, even though all the cases were always presented as exceptions. I wondered if there was anyone who seriously believed in the possibility that the model could be achieved in practice. I slowly came to realize, however, that most people in the NGO did. (Hilhorst, 2003, pp 121–122)

The fact that the model was being promoted internally within the NGO and not simply in reports to donors demonstrated that the NGO workers were gaining some kind of benefit from believing in the linear model, despite their own experience that it never functioned as it was supposed to function. In other words, the model clearly *worked* for the NGO practitioners in some way. Hilhorst concluded that the model worked in that it provided an anchor and a guideline to assist with decision-making; it helped to establish routines; it provided a language for making sense of and communicating the work; and, above all, it played a symbolic role in letting NGO workers believe that they were making progress towards an end goal.

Similarly, Goddard and Assad (2006) found, in their study of audit in Tanzanian NGOs that I referred to above, that the purpose of 'navigating legitimacy' in their case study was not merely to produce an image for outsiders, although this was probably the most important function. There was also a 'deeper moral base' where controls such as accounting mechanisms were internalised within the organisation, despite their lack of utility in a functional sense (ibid., p. 387).

When I asked about the idealisation of ALPS in ActionAid, one former staff member commented that this was 'in part due to a genuine desire in the sector to seek ways of working linked to values and principles – as the gulf widens between what organisations purport to stand for and what happens in practice, the need for myths and stories persists to inspire and encourage those who want to work in different ways. That's certainly the case in ActionAid'.

Are optics more important than reality?

So, NGOs are strongly incentivised to keep up appearances for reasons of external and internal legitimacy.

But there's more. I found in my research, which also resonates with my experience, that the optics related to concepts like NGO accountability or localisation can be, at times, more important for NGOs than actually achieving these aims on the ground.

Some authors writing in the broader NGO literature have raised the point that NGO work can have powerful symbolic benefits that may become more of a priority to achieve than the NGO's stated goals. These writings raise the question of what it means for development interventions to work or not work, to succeed or fail. David Mosse (2004, p. 18, 2005), in his ethnography in India, found that 'success' and 'failure' were related to the representation of the concept of the project rather than its actual operations on the ground:

> Ultimately what secured rising success for this project (in 1994–6) was neither a series of trivial participatory events ([participatory rural appraisals] etc.), nor even the delivery of quality physical programmes. Rather, success depended upon the donor-supported (and consultant elaborated) theory that linked participation/farmer control on the one hand, and better, more effective/sustainable programmes on the other.

Correspondingly, Mosse (2005, p. 21) found that, at a later stage, the project became 'vulnerable to "failure" not because of its practice, but because a new (ODA)[34] policy environment, made it harder for the project to articulate with the pre-occupations and ambitions of its donor supporters and interlocutors'.

David Lewis (2017) cited Mosse's case study in an article exploring the concept of 'organisational failure' in which he presented various ways in which organisations may 'succeed' even when it would appear that they are failing in terms of what they ostensibly set out to achieve. Lewis (2017) cited the work of Seibel (1999), who highlighted instances in which organisations continue to function and mobilise resources despite appearing to 'fail'. This happens 'not because they are "successful" in the conventional sense, but because they serve wider contextual political purposes – for example, they maintain the illusion that something is being done about an issue, they placate a potentially disruptive political constituency, or they serve a particular ideological purpose' (Lewis, 2017, p. 127). Seibel (1999, cited in Lewis, 2017, p. 127) called these 'successful failures'.

Another example in the literature was Zoe Marriage's case study of NGOs in South Sudan, which included a (non-income generating) income generation project. Marriage (2007, p. 498) outlined some benefits to donors and NGOs of creating a discourse of 'humanitarianism', quite apart from its implementation:

> There are benefits for donor countries in institutionalizing a political morality – framed by rights and principles – for providing assistance to civilians who are not important to geostrategic concerns. The calculated function of this political morality is to provide shared terminology for a perspective that serves the international hierarchy, including NGOs, which are funded and justified by it. This ensures the psychological well-being of aid staff and the political interests of the organizations.

Marriage further noted that while the projects themselves may not meet their stated objectives, the symbolic realm of the NGO projects was non-negotiable: 'Whilst NGOs discard their objectives at implementation, they cannot abandon them in principle. NGOs do not enjoy the financial or operational independence they claim, but more significantly, the weight of donors' political morality means that NGOs do not retain conceptual independence either — to disavow "humanitarianism" would be ideological blasphemy' (Marriage, 2007, p. 494).

In other words, nobody expected the NGO project objectives to be reached in this case, but the language surrounding the non-viable efforts was important and served other unstated objectives which, as Marriage noted, had both external and internal legitimacy benefits. The language may not be meaningful in terms of leading to any tangible results, but it keeps the show of the international aid sector on the road. Thus, the appearance of doing something is important, even if the work is not having much, or any, impact.

Importantly, I don't think that this analysis is necessarily casting judgements that all these projects mentioned were poor in reality – but more that whether they were good or bad in actuality was not the most relevant point in terms of what was making them succeed or fail; the key point rather was how they were being represented.

Another way, and a more positive way, of putting this is that projects can succeed (or fail) in different ways for different people. I have shown the significant symbolic power of ALPS and downward accountability for ActionAid in terms of legitimacy.

Even though ALPS appeared, from my case study, to be largely failing in terms of downward accountability, it appeared to be succeeding in other symbolic ways, which may have been even more important for the organisation.

When I realised this towards the end of my research, that representation could be more important than reality for NGOs, it made me see that this was another fundamental obstacle to NGOs achieving accountability to intended beneficiaries: for some actors, perhaps subconsciously, the symbolic value of putting in place downward accountability systems may outweigh the practical value. In other words, ALPS may have been more important as a representation than as an actual practice in terms of the internal and external legitimacy benefits that the organisation reaped from it. Hence, the incentive to ensure actual implementation of the stated goals may have diminished, since the benefits were already being achieved.

Lesson 9: In a context of managerialism, NGOs are incentivised to work on what's good for perceptions; but focusing on perceptions can reduce the incentive to act for goals like localisation.

I will come back to this point on optics and what can be done about it in the final chapter.

Before that, in the penultimate chapter, I will discuss a final lesson on changes ActionAid made to its governance system and how these affected its accountability.

CHAPTER FIFTEEN
Accountability through governance

This chapter about my 10th and final lesson looks at a different aspect of ActionAid's accountability: the ground-breaking internationalisation of its governance system. Harking back to my discussion earlier about definitions of accountability, an NGO's governance system is a place where legal authority exists, as opposed to just moral authority, and thus it interested me as a possible vehicle for improving accountability.

As part of the implementation of the 1999 *Fighting Poverty Together* strategy, the new internationalisation process in ActionAid began, running in parallel with the creation of ALPS. This process involved restructuring ActionAid 'from a loose alliance of agencies in Europe into a coherent international federation … so that its units in the developing countries of the "global South" could have an equal say in governance matters with units in wealthier nations of the "global North"' (ActionAid, 1999, pp. 1–2).

Moving from the previous situation where the organisation was governed by a UK-based board, internationalisation involved all ActionAid country offices, North and South, becoming self-governing, with their own general assemblies and boards, which were to send representatives to a new global general assembly and board, which would serve as the organisation's highest governing bodies. The *Taking Stock 3* governance review sets out the vision saying, 'The AAI Constitution of 2009 articulates a bold and visionary proposition: the re-distribution of organisational power in favour of people who are poor' (Fowler and Crane, 2010, p. 9).

Given its potential to enhance accountability to rights-holders, I included governance under the internationalisation process as part of my research. At international level, this was fairly light. I did a document review and interviewed the chair of the

ActionAid International board and a former board member, while including internationalisation as an interview topic with other stakeholders. In Uganda, I looked more in depth at the topic. I did a document review and interviewed four current and two former board members, as well as five General Assembly members. I also observed a national-level strategy meeting which included General Assembly members.

Governance at the international level

When I was doing my research, the governance structure that evolved during internationalisation had been much lauded and indeed I found that it was generally viewed positively by interviewees and in documents. It was said to constitute a significant shift of power from North to South that was aligning the organisation's structure more closely with its values. One current staff member commented, 'The new Governance structure is significant. It was a revelation in the [*People's Action to End Poverty 2012–2017*] strategy process how much input [General Assembly members] had. It's a wonderful shift of power and increase in democracy. This is a new accountability and needs to be embedded more'.

A study by Jayawickrama and Ebrahim (2013) found that most ActionAid International respondents felt that internationalisation had deepened the organisation's legitimacy and accountability.

A key consideration when it comes to assessing the downward accountability impact of the governance structure is to ask who is represented in the structure. At the time of my study, 6 of the 11 international board members were from developing countries, including the chair. This has now increased to 10 out of 12 (ActionAid, 2024b). Therefore, there is no doubt that the internationalisation process has made ActionAid's board significantly more Southern.

Governance in ActionAid Uganda

At the level of ActionAid Uganda, the first formal board of trustees was instituted in 2005. My research found that the board was strong, that it provided more oversight than existed before its establishment, and that it had helped ActionAid to become more legitimate and more 'Ugandan', as one interviewee put it, by bringing in strong Ugandan professionals from different sectors that played a role in decision-making for the country programme. The board was generally highly regarded by all stakeholders.

One contentious issue that emerged was that the board was voluntary, and thus some board members and former board members, during documented annual reviews, reported that the amount of work required made their voluntary participation difficult or impossible from a livelihood perspective. Given the voluntary nature of the board and the need for special skills in law, finance, human resources, and so on, it was unsurprising that the board was largely made up of upper-middle-class urban professionals, including some senior activists.

Thus, I found that the board did not play much of a role in directly enhancing accountability to intended beneficiaries by including poor people as members. Naturally, this did not prevent individual board members from consulting poor and marginalised groups to inform their work with ActionAid, and many board members were social activists in different ways.

The direct representation was apparently more the role of the General Assembly.

The evaluation of the country programme in 2010 was very positive on the General Assembly's role in enhancing downward accountability:

> The fact that partners have a stake in AAIU [ActionAid International Uganda] has therefore been a positive influence in the participation of AAIU's General Assembly members. That way AAIU has become more accountable to communities it works with. For example, the members of the General Assembly actively interrogate the Board on expenditure during the [Annual General Meeting] as well as follow through on previous plans that have been implemented (Kithinji et al., 2010, p. 32).

Another article co-written by a trustee and a staff member gave a similarly glowing review (Ovonji-Odida and Ogwal, 2009).

However, my research suggested a somewhat different interpretation to this view of the General Assembly, suggesting that there might be some brochure talk involved. As with my analysis of ALPS, I looked at transparency and participation as indicative of downward accountability. On the transparency front, the findings were very positive, Assembly members interviewed were unanimous that ActionAid was strong at providing them with timely and detailed documentation.

I then looked at the extent to which participation of intended beneficiaries influenced the decision-making of the General Assembly. To analyse this, I sought to determine: 1) who participated in the Assembly, 2) what decisions the Assembly made, and 3) how much influence different participants had within it.

In terms of who attended the Assembly, there was an effort made to include 'poor and marginalized' people, as per the goals of internationalisation (Ebrahim and Gordon, 2011, p. 6). According to my interviewees, partner representatives generally filled this role, making up half of the Assembly's 40 members. The partner Assembly members I interviewed told me that they attended the Assembly and engaged in open discussions on relevant topics such as the ActionAid strategies. It is worth recalling what I discussed above, that there are questions about how representative partners are of their own communities, but including partners in the governance structure still seemed like positive progress towards being more downwardly accountable.

Regarding the second issue of what the Assembly decides, the perspectives of interviewees were more negative. Some partners complained that the Assembly was merely a rubber-stamping body which does not go into the necessary level of detail on programming. One partner Assembly member commented, 'The General Assembly doesn't have power, we are not approving plans and budgets but receiving post-mortems like the annual accounts without the work plans. Things are over and we are only looking at one side. There were no plans so we couldn't feed into what money should be spent on x and y'.

Finally, on the third issue of how much influence partner members had within the Assembly, one problem that emerged was that partners often lacked the capacity to participate fully in the proceedings as they were from small, weak organisations and lacked skills and experience to interact in such fora. One board member said, 'The partners are reserved in the General Assembly they are not speaking out, they fear management more than the board. They are on their Sunday best. They don't want to jeopardise their relationship with [ActionAid]'. ActionAid Uganda recognised this capacity issue and at the time of my research, was seeking ways to build the capacity of Assembly members (Ojiambo, 2012).

Rights of authority

Thus, when I looked at country-level governance in some detail, particularly by interviewing representatives, it was a more mixed and complex picture than the documents had suggested and there were issues of power, capacity, and representativeness. I nevertheless felt that ActionAid's internationalisation process was a significant positive step for its downward accountability, not least because it gave partners and Ugandan board members (even if not usually poor and marginalised people themselves) more information and more potential to influence the organisation.

Critically, this is because being part of the governance system provides the 'rights of authority' that Mulgan (2000, p. 555) speaks about in his definition of accountability. As Brett (1993) notes, NGOs' attempts at empowerment which consist only of providing information and complaints mechanisms, engaging in participatory planning, and so on, depend on good will and do not give intended beneficiaries any independent authority.

I spoke earlier about NGO definitions of accountability revolving around *moral authority* or, in other words, a more *voluntary accountability* by NGOs. Obrecht (2011) and Mulgan (2003, p. 137) considered the concept of voluntary accountability a contradiction in terms, with the latter seeing it as detrimental as, when 'the recipients of charity have no recognised rights to complain or demand redress or otherwise hold the volunteers accountable, such grace-and-favour sensitivity by volunteers hardly counts as accountability at all. To describe it as such only serves to hide the lack of external scrutiny and remedies that pervades the non profit [*sic*] sector'.

In transforming its governance system to give away some real authority and power, ActionAid was attempting to go beyond this 'grace-and-favour sensitivity'. It was obviously crucial how this was implemented and what I saw in Uganda needed some improvements. It was easy for tokenism to emerge. But I found it a worthwhile attempt that had potential.

Lesson 10: An NGO interested in improving its downward accountability should take a serious look at what can be done within its own governance system, where real shifts in authority can occur, as long as implementation is carefully monitored and tokenism avoided.

I will now move to the conclusion of this book and some final recommendations.

CHAPTER SIXTEEN
Conclusion and the way forward

I think some of the most important things I learnt in the research and practice I talk about in this book were related to myself. When I started my work on partnership and downward accountability, I was keen to help NGOs fix things to improve their relationships with communities. I was very solutions-focused and action-oriented. These sound like positive traits, but they aren't if you don't have an adequate understanding of what you are trying to solve and act upon!

In particular, when I started my PhD, I was impatient to get to the part where I made recommendations. It took a while, and a lot of patience and guidance from my PhD supervisor, for me to realise that I needed to read and think and understand a lot more widely and deeply before presuming to make recommendations. What's more, recommendations are most useful when they are tailored to a particular geographical and organisational context. This is why this book is quite light on recommendations. Rather, I hope that most of the usefulness of this book will be in its 10 lessons helping practitioners to understand and analyse their situations better, and to figure out for themselves how to move forward. Nevertheless, in this chapter, I will give two broad recommendations that might be helpful. First, I will give a quick recap of the 10 lessons.

Partnership-related lessons

The first four lessons relate loosely to partnership, although they could equally apply to any aspect of localisation. The first is that partnership needs to be planned with careful attention to the context. Having worked in some contexts with extremely strong local civil society actors (such as India) and others with very weak NGOs (such as South Sudan), I learnt how radically different the approaches of international supporters need to be. The second lesson is related but can be a bit controversial, which is that partnership with local organisations is not always an appropriate way to support localisation. There may be better ways to reach and support local communities, again depending on the context. And we should not let political correctness stand in the way of figuring out how localisation should look in different contexts.

The third lesson is that with partnership, or indeed any localisation initiative, we should be careful who claims to speak for the community and how they engage with wider groups of community members. Finally, the fourth lesson is that we need to challenge the notion that partnership or localisation will necessarily allow international organisations to immediately reduce their staffing. Again, depending on the context, localisation will need different kinds of support from the international organisation and both the quantity and types of staff are important to consider if the organisation is serious about supporting localisation.

Lessons on obstacles to watch out for

The second grouping – the fifth through tenth lessons – could be termed obstacles to localisation that may not be obvious, but that organisations need to watch out for in order to address them and avoid the related pitfalls. The first of these, the fifth lesson, is about power dynamics. These are everywhere: within NGOs themselves; between international and national or local NGOs; between NGOs and communities; and within communities. There are lots of different implications of the various permutations of power dynamics, but the first step is to seek to understand how these dynamics are manifesting themselves in different situations where localisation is being attempted. Appropriate action can then follow. The sixth lesson is about trend-jumping – the tendency of NGOs to jump on the latest fad in the sector, rather than seriously implement initiatives. I provide some guidance for how to detect trend-jumping and what to avoid if localisation is not just to be the latest trend for an organisation.

The seventh lesson is about the pressures on and interests of individual NGO staff members and how this can shape their engagement in localisation initiatives – this is an important area which gets far too little attention when initiatives are being planned. The eighth lesson is about NGOs' (conscious or unconscious) tendency to want to retain control over their programming, which can be an obstacle to really submitting themselves to what localisation might mean in terms of programming decisions. I then suggest with the ninth lesson that NGOs need to watch out for optics as a powerful incentive for inaction. In other words, the optics benefit can sometimes reduce the incentive for real progress in areas like localisation, if benefits can be gained simply by the appearance of progress.

The tenth lesson is a bit different; it highlights the positive example of reforms to ActionAid's governance system to illustrate that an NGO's governance structure can have potential to enhance its downward accountability, while flagging some potential obstacles to avoid, such as tokenism.

What all this means for NGOs

So where do the findings in the book leave NGOs when planning for localisation? Apart from acting on the basis of these 10 lessons, is there anything else that can be said on how NGOs can navigate more constructive paths to better serve intended beneficiaries?

I will conclude with two broad recommendations. First, that NGOs should be careful with their language to avoid getting caught up in optics. And second that NGOs should consider limiting their growth if they want to really invest in and be close to the communities they set out to serve.

Take care with language to confront the optics issue

I have made a case for why the prioritisation of optics in the aid sector is so likely, as it boosts an organisation's external and internal legitimacy. And I have talked about how this can disincentivise progress on localisation.

So, what can NGOs do about this?

My recommendation here is that NGOs should pay close attention to the language they use to avoid getting caught up in optics at the expense of real progress. I discussed earlier how language in the aid sector can be opaque, rhetorical, and exclusive, often perpetuating the status quo. In a paper on whether poor people are mobilised by anti-poverty programmes, Joshi and Moore (2000) concluded that aid organisations' ways of working are often disempowering in themselves, even while they are trying to implement empowerment programmes. The authors noted that the 'genuine inability to see through the fog of fashionable jargon and to think clearly about the political and institutional issues may be part of the problem' (ibid., p. 26).

NGOs should try to recognise and be conscious of their own brochure talk and the idealised language that may have emerged around their practices, and they should work towards frank internal discussions that more closely reflect staff (including local-level staff) experiences of actual practices. As Sogge and Biekart (1996, p. 201) noted in a discussion on NGO claims regarding their impact, NGOs have 'the choice to stop fooling themselves...Out of the glare of the public media, agencies can take long sober looks at their activities and draw conclusions about the norms and paradigms that have guided them up to now'.

Breaking out of what one ActionAid staff member called the 'jargon-driven malaise' that often afflicts NGO work will allow organisations to reflect, with perhaps more honesty and modesty than usual, on how they want to move forward with their goals. The fog lifting is the first step!

Align funding structures with the goal of supporting transformative change at community level

My second recommendation concerns NGOs' funding structures. I found in my study that the desire for external legitimacy, particularly vis-à-vis donors, was a central reason for the continuation of the disjuncture between what NGOs say and what they actually do. Getting practices closer to aims would require considerable shifts in funding structures for most organisations.

A 2015 article by Banks et al. (2015, p. 715) revisiting earlier work on whether NGOs and donors are 'too close for comfort' touched on a number of themes that resonated a lot with what I discuss in this book. The authors were critical of the de-politicisation of development in the work of the aid system in general and professional NGOs in particular, noting that the system 'continues to overlook the systems, processes, and institutions that reproduce poverty and inequality'. Similar to the reflections of David Mosse, Banks et al. (2015, p. 710, citing Balboa, 2014) noted the inherent contradiction between the NGO fundraising imperatives and actions that are really engaging with local communities: 'the attributes that make transnational NGOs successful in mobilizing large sums of funding and influencing policy at the same time set them up for failure when it comes to creating lasting, meaningful, and context specific change on the ground'.

Banks et al. (2015, p. 715) proposed that NGOs should engage far more deeply with the political economy of social change, should work with member-based organisations and social movements, and 'retreat from the idea that transformation is simply the aggregate of technical interventions (Carothers & de Gramont, 2013; Green, 2008)'. While I would certainly agree with their proposition in principle, as I have noted earlier, organisations like ActionAid have often set out to do just that, and there is a wide spectrum of the availability of such social movements in different contexts.

However, the key point here is that, regardless of the baseline level of member-based organisations or social movements in a community, if an organisation chooses to aim for transformative approaches on poverty and marginalisation, chooses to *walk the talk* on being more community-centred and community-driven, this will require a lot of effort. The organisation will need to find ways to invest significant resources and time at the community level; to commit for the long term; to take risks; and to continuously reflect and be prepared to change priorities as the context changes and as new opportunities or challenges arise. This kind of work is not easily scalable, given that it requires so much investment in staffing in particular communities.

Critically, to make the necessary kinds of investments at community level, an organisation will need to look carefully at its funding structures. It should only accept funds based on conditions and requirements that will not compromise its relationships with communities – whether that means negotiating with existing donors or finding new ways to raise funds. In a paper on the future of accountability within ActionAid, one international staff member wrote: 'In the pursuit of money to sustain our organisations and staff we may be in danger of wandering down a road of political compromise. Or is there another path we can seek? The shape of the alternative is not entirely clear to me but features smaller budgets based on "cleaner" funds that allow us to continue to fulfil our mission and our work with integrity' (Hargreaves, 2009, p. 38).

An organisation which does not already have significant flexible funding may find that it is impossible to survive with this new approach to its funding, or they may find that it is possible to survive but that the organisation must remain small and, possibly, institutionally insecure.

The aim here should be to align an organisation's structure as closely as possible with its goals. As Banks et al. (2015, p. 715) conclude: 'only by acknowledging, confronting and challenging the problems that NGOs face in the international aid chain can we move toward relationships that are more supportive of NGO autonomy and a greater diversity of civil society action'.

This agenda will require much self-reflection within individual organisations. Refusing potential funding opportunities and remaining small would be counter-intuitive for most organisations and would work against their desires to create a more sustainable organisational base, to assure job security for staff, to pay their rent, and so on. As Banks et al. (ibid., p.715) note, such a change 'will challenge the identity of NGOs and their willingness to be judged by criteria other than their own size and profile'. But such challenges and risks are likely necessary in order for organisations to maintain their independence to pursue genuinely transformative community-driven work, if that is indeed their goal.

References

ActionAid (1999) *Fighting Poverty Together: ActionAid's Strategy 1999–2003*. London: ActionAid. Available at: https://actionaid. org/publications/1999/fighting-poverty-together-actionaids-strategy-1999-2005

ActionAid (2000) *Accountability Learning and Planning System*. London: ActionAid International.

ActionAid (2004) *Management Response to the Reports 2004*. Johannesburg: ActionAid International.

ActionAid (2005) *Rights to End Poverty: ActionAid International Strategy 2005–10*. Johannesburg: ActionAid International. Available at: https://actionaid.org/publications/2005/rights-end-poverty-actionaid-international-strategy-2005-2010

ActionAid (2006a) *Accountability Learning and Planning System*. Johannesburg: ActionAid International.

ActionAid (2006b) *Exchanges: Sharing our Lessons on ALPS Grounding*. Johannesburg: ActionAid International.

ActionAid (2007) *ALPS Review 2007*. Johannesburg: ActionAid International.

ActionAid (2009) *ActionAid International/DFID PPA 'LOGICAL FRAMEWORK'*. Johannesburg: ActionAid International.

ActionAid (2010a) *Development Areas (DAs): An Internal Audit Report on the State of Affairs*. Johannesburg: ActionAid International.

ActionAid (2010b) *Making Sense of International Initiatives in Accountability; Positioning Action Aid International*. Johannesburg: ActionAid International.

ActionAid (2010c) *Taking Stock Review 3: Self Review Format: IDs Input*. Johannesburg: ActionAid International.

ActionAid (2011a) *People's Action to End Poverty: ActionAid's Strategy 2012–2017*. Johannesburg: ActionAid International. Available at: https://actionaid.org/publications/2011/peoples-action-end-poverty

ActionAid (2011b) *Risk Management Report*. Johannesburg: ActionAid International.

ActionAid (2012) *Financial Report and Accounts 2011*. Johannesburg: ActionAid International.

ActionAid (2013) 'What We Do'. Available at: https://web.archive. org/web/20130205173124/https://actionaid.org/what-we-do

ActionAid (2024a) *Annual Report 2023: Hope & Humanity*. Johannesburg: ActionAid. Available at: https://actionaid.org/ publications/2024/annual-report-2023-hope-humanity

ActionAid (2024b) 'International board members'. Available at: https://actionaid.org/international-board-members

ActionAid (2024c) 'Who we are'. Available at: https://actionaid.org/ who-we-are

ActionAid Kenya (2006) *Mwangaza*. Kisumu: ActionAid Kenya.

ActionAid Kenya (2010) *Using Transparency Boards to Promote, Upward, Downward and Social Accountability: The case of AAIK*. Nairobi: ActionAid Kenya.

ActionAid Nepal (2006) *ActionAid Nepal Study of ALPS*. Kathmandu: ActionAid Nepal.

ActionAid Nepal (2010) *Social Audit: A Bold Step Towards Promoting Accountability and Transparency: A Story of Change from ActionAid Nepal*. Kathmandu: ActionAid Nepal.

ActionAid Uganda (1994) *AAU Management Summary 1995 Plan and Budget*. Kampala: ActionAid Uganda.

ActionAid Uganda (2000) *ActionAid Uganda: Country Programme Review Report*. Kampala: ActionAid Uganda.

ActionAid Uganda (2001) *Annual Report 2000*. Kampala: ActionAid Uganda.

ActionAid Uganda (2002) *Annual Report 2001*. Kampala: ActionAid Uganda.

ActionAid Uganda (2004) *ActionAid Uganda Annual Report 2003*. Kampala: ActionAid Uganda.

ActionAid Uganda (2005a) *OD/HR Newsletter Vol 1 Issue 4*. Kampala: ActionAid Uganda.

ActionAid Uganda (2005b) *Participatory Review and Reflection Process (PRRP) Report 2004*. Kampala: ActionAid Uganda.

ActionAid Uganda (2005c) *Rights Access and Justice: A Strategy for Transformation. Country Strategic Plan 3*. Kampala: ActionAid Uganda.

ActionAid Uganda (2006) *Katakwi DI Audit 2006*. Kampala: ActionAid Uganda.

ActionAid Uganda (2007) *Katakwi DI Annual Report 2006*. Kampala: ActionAid Uganda.

ActionAid Uganda (2009a) *AAIU Internal Audit Report, 2009*. Kampala: ActionAid Uganda.

ActionAid Uganda (2009b) *ActionAid Annual Report 2008*. Kampala: ActionAid Uganda.

ActionAid Uganda (2011) *2011 Audit Query Matrix*. Kampala: ActionAid Uganda.

ActionAid Uganda (2012a) *ActionAid Uganda Internal Audit Report February 2012*. Kampala: ActionAid Uganda.

ActionAid Uganda (2012b) *Annual Report 2011*. Kampala: ActionAid International Uganda.

ActionAid Uganda (2013) *Annual Report 2012*. Kampala: ActionAid Uganda.

Agyemang, G. Awumbila, M., Unerman, J., and O'Dwyer, B. (2009) *NGO Accountability and Aid Delivery*. London: The Association of Chartered Certified Accountants.

Aristotle (1991) *On Rhetoric: A Theory of Civic Discourse, translated by G.A. Kennedy*. New York: Oxford University Press.

Apthorpe (2016) 'Alice in Aidland', unpublished

Baguios, A., King, M., Martins, A., and Pinnington, R. (2021) *Are We There Yet? Localisation as the Journey Towards Locally Led Practice*. ODI Report. London: ODI. Available at: https://odi.org/en/publications/are-we-there-yet-localisation-as-the-journey-towards-locally-led-practice/

Banks, N., Hulme, D. and Edwards, M. (2015) 'NGOs, States, and Donors Revisited: Still Too Close for Comfort?', *World Development*, 66, pp. 707–718. https://doi.org/10.1016/j.worlddev.2014.09.028

Barbelet, V., Davies, G., Flint, J., and Davey, E. (2021) *Interrogating the Evidence Base on Humanitarian Localisation: A Literature Study*. HPG literature review. London: ODI. Available at: https://odi.org/en/publications/interrogating-the-evidence-base-on-humanitarian-localisation-a-literature-study/

Baur, D. and Schmitz, H.P. (2012) 'Corporations and NGOs: When Accountability Leads to Co-optation', *Journal of Business Ethics*, 106, pp. 9–21. https://doi.org/10.1007/s10551-011-1057-9

Bendell, J. (2006) *Debating NGO Accountability*. New York and Geneva: United Nations Non-Governmental Liaison Service.

Bertin, L. (2004) *Taking Stock II – Synthesis Report 2004*. Johannesburg: ActionAid International.

Blagescu, M. and Lloyd, R. (2006) *Global Accountability Report: Holding Power to Account*. London: One World Trust.

Bonbright, D. and Batliwala, S. (2007) 'Answering for Ourselves: Accountability for Citizen Organisations'. *Civicus World Assembly*, Glasgow.

Bornstein, E. (2005) *The Spirit of Development: Protestant NGOs, Morality and Economics in Zimbabwe*. Stanford: Stanford University Press.

Brehm, V.M., Harris-Curtis, E., Padrao, L., and Tanner, M. (2004) *Autonomy or Dependence? Case Studies of North-South NGO Partnerships*. Oxford: INTRAC. Available at: https://www.intrac.org/resources/autonomy-dependence-case-studies-north-south-ngo-partnerships/

Brett, E.A. (1993) 'Voluntary agencies as development organisations: theorising the problem of efficiency and accountability', *Development and Change*, 24, 24, pp. 269–303. https://doi.org/10.1111/j.1467-7660.1993.tb00486.x

Brown, L.D. (2008) *Creating Credibility: Legitimacy and Accountability for Transnational Civil Society*. Sterling, VA: Kumarian Press.

Brown, L.D. (2010) *Taking Stock Review 3*. Johannesburg: ActionAid International.

Brown, L.D. and Jagadananda (2007) *Civil Society Legitimacy and Accountability: Issues and Challenges*. Cambridge, MA: Hauser Centre for Nonprofit Organization and Civicus.

Chambers, R. (1996) 'The Primacy of the Personal', in M. Edwards and D. Hulme (eds) *Beyond the Magic Bullet: NGO Performance and Accountability in the Post-Cold War World*. West Hartford, CT: Kumarian Press.

Chapman, J., David, R. and Mancini, A. (2003) 'Transforming Practice in Action Aid: Experiences and Challenges in Rethinking Learning, Monitoring and Accountability Systems', in L. Earle (ed.) *Creativity and Constraint*. Oxford: INTRAC.

Clark, J. (1991) *Democratizing Development: The Role of Voluntary Organizations*. Boulder, CO: Lynne Rienner Publishers.

Concern Worldwide (1998) *Strategic Plan 1997–2002*. Dublin: Concern Worldwide.

Concern Worldwide (2002) *Strategic Plan, March 2002 – March 2005*. Dublin: Concern Worldwide.

Cooke, B. and Kothari, U. (2001) *Participation, The New Tyranny?* London: Zed Books.

Cornwall, A. and Brock, K. (2005) *Beyond Buzzwords: "Poverty Reduction", "Participation" and "Empowerment" in Development Policy*. Geneva: United Nations Research Institute for Social Development.

David, R. and Mancini, A. (2003) 'Transforming development practice – the journey in the quest to develop planning, monitoring and evaluation systems that facilitate (rather than hinder) development'. *37th meeting of the Working Party on Aid Evaluation*, Paris, 27 March.

David, R. and Mancini, A. (2004) *Going Against the Flow: The Struggle to Make Organisational Systems Part of the Solution Rather than Part of the Problem: The Case of Action Aid's Accountability, Learning and Planning System,* IDS Organisational Learning Series [Preprint], (7).

David, R. and Mancini, A. (2011) 'Participation, Learning and Accountability: The Role of the Activist Academic', in A. Cornwall and I. Scoones (eds) *Revolutionizing Development: Reflections on the Work of Robert Chambers.* London: Earthscan.

David, R., Mancini, A. and Guijt, I. (2006) 'Bringing Systems in Line with Values: The Practice of the Accountability, Learning and Planning System (ALPS)', in R. Eyben (ed.) *Relationships for Aid.* London: Zed Books.

DENIVA (2006) *Civil Society in Uganda: At the Crossroads?* Kampala: CIVICUS.

Dichter, T. (1999) *ActionAid Taking Stock Review: Summary Report.* London: ActionAid International.

DiMaggio, P.J. and Powell, W.W. (1983) 'The Iron Cage Revisited: Institutional Isomorphism and Collective Rationality in Organizational Fields', *American Sociological Review,* 48(2), pp. 147–60. https://doi.org/10.2307/2095101

Drabek, A.G. (1987) 'Development Alternatives: The Challenge for NGOs – An Overview of the Issues', *World Development,* 15(Supplement 1), pp. ix–xv. https://doi.org/10.1016/0305-750X(87)90135-5

Ebrahim, A. and Gordon, R. (2011) *ActionAid International: Globalizing Governance, Localizing Accountability.* Cambridge, MA: Harvard Business School.

Ebrahim, A. and Weisband, E. (2007) 'Introduction: Forging Global Accountabilities', in A. Ebrahim and E. Weisband (eds) *Global Accountabilities. Participation, Pluralism and Public Ethics.* Cambridge: Cambridge University Press.

Edwards, M. and Hulme, D. (1996) *Beyond the Magic Bullet: NGO Performance and Accountability in the Post-Cold War World.* West Hartford, CT: Kumarian Press.

Elbers, W. and Schulpen, L. (2011) 'Decision Making in Partnerships for Development: Explaining the Influence of Local Partners', *Nonprofit and Voluntary Sector Quarterly,* 40(5), pp. 795–812. https://doi.org/10.1177/0899764010366304

Etim, J.S. (2016) 'Private universities in Nigeria: Prevalence, course offerings, cost, and manpower development', in M. Shah and C.S. Nair (eds) *A Global Perspective on Private Higher Education.* Chandos Publishing, pp. 271–286. https://doi.org/10.1016/B978-0-08-100872-0.00016-1

European Commission (no date) *Logical Framework – Logframe, EXACT External Wiki*. Available at: https://wikis.ec.europa.eu/display/ExactExternalWiki/Logical+Framework+-+Logframe

Eyben, R. (2006) *Relationships for Aid*. London: Earthscan.

Ferretti, S. (2007) 'Accountability and Learning: Finding the Balance'. *MAPS Learning Forum*, Dublin, 28 November.

Fowler, A. (ed.) (1997) *Striking a Balance: A Guide to Enhancing the Effectiveness of Non-Governmental Organisations in International Development*. London: Routledge. https://doi.org/10.4324/9781315070735

Fowler, A. (2000) *Partnerships: Negotiating relationships – A Resource for Non-governmental Development Organisations*. INTRAC occasional papers series no. 32. Oxford: INTRAC.

Fowler, A. (2005) *Aid Architecture: Reflections on NGDO Futures and the Emergence of Counter-Terrorism*. INTRAC occasional papers series no.45. Oxford: INTRAC. Available at: https://www.researchgate.net/publication/245236135_Aid_Architecture_Reflections_on_NGDO_Futures_and_the_Emergence_of_Counter-Terrorism

Fowler, A.F. and Crane, W. (2010) *Taking Stock 3: Governance, Human Resources and Organisational Development*. Johannesburg: ActionAid International.

Frennesson, L., Kembro, J., de Vries, H., Jahre, M., and Van Wassenhove, L. (2022) 'International humanitarian organizations' perspectives on localization efforts', *International Journal of Disaster Risk Reduction*, 83, 103410. https://doi.org/10.1016/j.ijdrr.2022.103410

Goddard, A. and Assad, M.J. (2006) 'Accounting and navigating legitimacy in Tanzanian NGOs', *Accounting, Auditing & Accountability Journal*, 19(3), pp. 377–404. https://doi.org/10.1108/09513570610670343

Goetz, A.M. and Jenkins, R. (2002) *Voice, Accountability and Human Development: The Emergence of a New Agenda*. New York: United Nations Development Programme.

Gottlieb, A. (2006) 'Ethnography: Theory and Methods', in E. Perecman and S.R. Curran (eds) *A Handbook for Social Science Field Research*. Thousand Oaks, CA: Sage Publications.

Grand Bargain (2023a) *Grand Bargain Beyond 2023 Framework*. Grand Bargain. Available at: https://interagencystandingcommittee.org/sites/default/files/migrated/2023-06/Grand%20Bargain%20beyond%202023%20-%20Framework.pdf

Grand Bargain (2023b) 'Grand Bargain Signatories'. Available at: https://interagencystandingcommittee.org/node/22229

Grand Bargain (2024) *Localisation Learning Space: Progressing Towards 25% Direct Funding to Local and National Actors*. Grand Bargain.

Available at: https://interagencystandingcommittee.org/grand-bargain-official-website/localisation-learning-space-progressing-towards-25-direct-funding-local-and-national-actors-0

Grand Bargain (2025a) *Implementation Agenda 2024–2026.* Available at: https://interagencystandingcommittee.org/grand-bargain-official-website/implementation-agenda-2024-2026-en-fr-sp-ar

Grand Bargain (2025b) The Grand Bargain [website]. Available at: https://interagencystandingcommittee.org/grand-bargain

Grand Bargain Secretariat (2016) *The Grand Bargain – A Shared Commitment to Better Serve People in Need.* Istanbul, Turkey. Available at: https://interagencystandingcommittee.org/sites/default/files/migrated/2016-06/the_grand_bargain_may_2016.pdf

Gugerty, M.K. (2010) 'The emergence and design of NGO clubs in Africa', in M.K. Gugerty and A. Prakash (eds) *Voluntary Regulation of NGOs and Nonprofits: An Accountability Club Framework.* Cambridge: Cambridge University Press.

Guijt, I. (2004) *ALPS in Action: A Review of the Shift in ActionAid towards a new Accountability, Learning and Planning System.* Taking Stock II. ActionAid International. Available at: https://www.researchgate.net/publication/40121988_ALPS_in_Action_A_Review_of_the_Shift_in_ActionAid_towards_a_new_Accountability_Learning_and_Planning_System

Guijt, I. (2007) *Critical Readings on Assessing and Learning for Social Change: A Review.* Brighton: IDS.

Gulrajani, N. (2011) 'Transcending the great foreign aid debate: Managerialism, radicalism and the search for aid effectiveness', *Third World Quarterly*, 32(2), pp. 199–216. https://doi.org/10.1080/01436597.2011.560465

Harding, D. (2013) 'Taking our lead from reality – an open practice for social development', in T. Wallace and F. Porter (eds) *Aid, NGOs and the Realities of Women's Lives: A Perfect Storm.* Rugby: Practical Action.

Hargreaves, S. (2009) 'The Politics of Accountability in Our Struggles for Rights and Justice', *Exchanges on Accountability: Newsletter of the IASL Community* [Preprint], (4).

Harris, M.J. (2011) 'Strategic Planning in an International Nongovernmental Development Organization: The Creation of a Meta-Identity', *Administration and Society*, 43(2), pp. 216–247. https://doi.org/10.1177/0095399711400052

Hately, L. (1997) 'The Power of Partnership', in L. Hately and K. Malhotra, *Between Rhetoric and Reality: Essays on Partnership in Development.* Ottawa: North-South Institute, pp. 3–36.

Helman, C. and Moore, P. (2002) *ActionAid Kenya – Organisation Development Case Study*. Nairobi: ActionAid International.

Hewitt Associates (2010) *Employee Engagement Survey Results Uganda*. Kampala: ActionAid.

Hilhorst, D. (2003) *The Real World of NGOs: Discourses, Diversity and Development*. London: Zed.

Holloway, R. (1998) *Supporting Citizens' Initiatives: Bangladesh's NGOs and Society*. London : Intermediate Technology Publications.

Humanitarian Accountability Partnership (2013) 'What is accountability?' Available at: https://web.archive.org/web/20130429093005/http://www.hapinternational.org/about/what-is-accountability.aspx

IASL (Impact Assessment and Shared Learning) (2010) *Impact Assessment and Shared Learning Self Review*. Johannesburg: ActionAid International.

Ical, F. and Leon, R. (2009) 'AA Guatemala and Participatory Budgeting: An Empowering Practice', *Exchanges* [Preprint].

Imam, A. (2010) *ActionAid International Taking Stock 3: Women's Rights Internationally and Africa Regions*. Johannesburg: ActionAid International.

Ireri, B. (2010) 'Using Transparency Boards to Achieve Upward, Downward and Social Accountability: The Case of AAIK'. *Reimagining Accountability*, Brighton: Institute of Development Studies, University of Sussex.

Jayawickrama, S. and Ebrahim, A. (2013) *Building and Governing a Democratic Federation: The ActionAid International Story*. Boston, MA: Hauser Center for Nonprofit Organizations, Harvard University.

Jordan, L. (2005) *Mechanisms for NGO Accountability*. Cambridge: Global Public Policy Institute.

Jordan, L. (2007) 'A rights-based approach to accountability', in A. Ebrahim and E. Weisband (eds) *Global Accountabilities: Participation, Pluralism and Public Ethics*. Cambridge: Cambridge University Press, pp. 151–167.

Joshi, A. and Moore, M. (2000) 'Enabling Environments: Do Antipoverty Programs Mobilize the Poor?', *The Journal of Development Studies*, 37(1), pp. 25–56. https://doi.org/10.1080/713600057

Kabenge, D., Mugisha, M., Magala, C., and Mpagi, T. (2005) *Uganda Country Programme Review*. Kampala: ActionAid Uganda.

KASDA (Kapujan Sub County Development Association) (2005) *KASDA Partner Appraisal and Assessment Questionnaire*. Kapujan Uganda: KASDA.

Kennedy, G.A. (2001) 'Rhetoric', in N.J. Smelser and P.B. Baltes (eds) *International Encyclopedia of the Social & Behavioral Sciences*. Amsterdam: Elsevier Science Limited.

Keystone and AccountAbility (2006) *A BOND Approach to Quality in Non-Governmental Organisations: Putting Beneficiaries First*. London: BOND.

Kilby, P. (2004a) 'Is Empowerment Possible Under a New Public Management Environment? Some Lessons from India', *International Public Management Journal*, 7(3), pp. 207–225.

Kilby, P. (2004b) 'Nongovernmental Organizations and Accountability in an Era of Global Anxiety', *Seton Hall Journal of Diplomacy and International Relations*, 5(2), pp. 67–78.

Kithinji, H., Nabachwa, M. and Wagubi, P. (2010) *AAIU CSP 3 Evaluation Report*. Kampala: ActionAid.

Koch, D.-J. (2008) 'A Paris Declaration for NGOs?', in *Financing Development 2008: Whose Ownership?* Paris: OECD, pp. 59–84.

Korten, D.C. (1990) *Getting to the 21st Century: Voluntary Action and the Global Agenda*. Boulder, CO: Lynne Rienner Publishers.

Kramer, R.M. (1981) *Voluntary Agencies in the Welfare State*. Berkeley, CA: University of California Press.

Laugharn, P. (2024) 'The time is right for donors to deliver on locally led development'. Devex, 24 July. Available at: https://www.devex.com/news/sponsored/opinion-the-time-is-right-for-donors-to-deliver-on-locally-led-development-108012.

Leach, M. (2010) *Summary Report: ActionAid External Stakeholder Assessment*. Washington, DC: Management Assistance Group.

Lewis, D. (2007) 'Bringing in society, culture and politics: Values and accountability in a Bangladeshi NGO', in A. Ebrahim and E. Weisband (eds) *Global Accountabilities: Participation, Pluralism and Public Ethics*. Cambridge: Cambridge University Press, pp. 131–147.

Lewis, D. (2013) 'Reconnecting development policy, people and history', in T. Wallace and F. Porter (eds) *Aid, NGOs and the Realities of Women's Lives*. Rugby: Practical Action Publishing.

Lewis, D. (2014) *Non-Governmental Organizations, Management and Development*, 3rd edn. London: Routledge. https://doi.org/10.4324/9780203591185

Lewis, D. (2017) 'When things go wrong in NGOs: What can be learned from cases of organizational breakdown and "failure"?', in I. Basu, J. Devine, and G. Wood (eds) *Politics and Governance in Bangladesh*. London: Routledge, pp. 125–142.

Lloyd, R., Oatham, J. and Hammer, M. (2007) *Global Accountability Report*. London: One World Trust.

Long, N. (2001) *Development Sociology: Actor Perspectives*. London: Routledge.

Lynch-Bell, M. (2012) *ActionAid Financial Report and Accounts 2011*. Johannesburg: ActionAid International.

Malhotra, K. (1997) '"Something Nothing" Words: Lessons in Partnership from Southern Experience', in L. Hately and K. Malhotra, *Between Rhetoric and Reality: Essays on Partnership in Development*. Ottawa: North South Institute, pp. 37–56.

Marriage, Z. (2007) 'Not breaking the rules, not playing the game: International assistance to countries at war', *Round table*, 388, pp. 79–80.

Merriam-Webster (2024) 'Definition of optics', *Merriam-Webster Dictionary*. Available at: https://www.merriam-webster.com/dictionary/optics

Mosse, D. (2004) 'Good Policy is Unimplementable? Reflections on the Ethnography of Aid Policy and Practice.', *Development and Change*, 35(4), pp. 639–671. https://doi.org/10.1111/j.0012-155X.2004.00374.x

Mosse, D. (2005) *Cultivating Development: An Ethnography of Aid Policy and Practice*. London: Pluto Press.

Mowles, C. (2013) 'Evaluation, complexity, uncertainty – theories of change and some alternatives', in T. Wallace and F. Porter (eds) *Aid, NGOs and the Realities of Women's Lives: A Perfect Storm*. Rugby: Practical Action.

Mulgan, R. (2000) '"Accountability": An Ever-Expanding Concept?', *Public Administration*, 78(3), pp. 555–573. https://doi.org/10.1111/1467-9299.00218

Mulgan, R. (2003) *Holding Power to Account: Accountability in Modern Democracies*. New York: Palgrave MacMillan.

Najam, A. (1996) 'NGO accountability: A conceptual framework', *Development Policy Review*, 14(4), pp. 339–353. https://doi.org/10.1111/j.1467-7679.1996.tb00112.x

Newman, K. (2011) *Challenges and Dilemmas in Integrating Human Rights Based Approaches and Participatory Approaches to Development: An Exploration of the Experiences of ActionAid International*. PhD Thesis. Goldsmiths College, University of London. Available at: https://research.gold.ac.uk/id/eprint/10563/

Obrecht, A. (2011) *Getting it Right: An Account of the Moral Agency of NGOs*. PhD Thesis. London School of Economics and Political Science. Available at: https://etheses.lse.ac.uk/163/

Ojiambo, L. (2012) *Handover Note: Board Liaison Officer – March 2012*. Kampala: ActionAid Uganda.

Okwaare, S. and Chapman, J. (2006) 'Chameleons and Accountability: Linking Learning with Increasing Accountability in Action Aid

International Uganda and the Ugandan Land Alliance', in L. Jordan and P. Van Tuijl (eds) *NGO Accountability*. London: Earthscan.

Omelicheva, M.Y. (2004) '"Global Civil Society?" An Empirical Portrayal'. *2004 Annual Meeting of the American Political Science Association, Chicago, 2–3 September*.

Ovonji-Odida, I. and Ogwal, H.N. (2009) 'Deepening Accountability through Nationalisation – The Ugandan Experience', *Exchanges on Accountability: Newsletter of the IASL Community* [Preprint], (4).

Pfeffer, J. and Salancik, G.R. (1978) *The External Control of Organizations: A Resource Dependence Perspective*. New York: Harper & Row.

Roberts, S.M., Jones, J.P.I. and Frohling, O. (2005) 'NGOs and the globalization of managerialism: A research framework', *World Development*, 33(11), pp. 1845–64. https://doi.org/10.1016/j.worlddev.2005.07.004

Robillard, S., Atim, T. and Maxwell, D. (2021) *Localization: A "Landscape" Report*. Boston, MA: Feinstein International Center, Tufts University. Available at: https://fic.tufts.edu/publication-item/localization-a-landscape-report/

Scott-Smith, T. (2013) 'Insulating the developing classes', in T. Wallace and F. Porter (eds) *Aid, NGOs and the Realties of Women's Lives: A Perfect Storm*. Rugby: Practical Action Publishing.

Scott-Villiers, P. (2002) 'The struggle for organisational change: How the ActionAid Accountability, Learning and Planning System emerged', *Development in Practice*, 12(3 & 4), pp. 424–435. https://doi.org/10.1080/0961450220149771

Seibel, W. (1999) 'Successful failure: an alternative view of organizational coping', in H. Anheier (ed.) *When Things Go Wrong: Organizational Failures and Breakdowns*. London: Sage.

Sellars, R. (2006) 'Rhetoric', *Theory, Culture & Society*, 23(2–3), pp. 59–60. https://doi.org/10.1177/026327640602300212

Shah, A. (2013) 'I don't know ... and related thoughts', in T. Wallace and F. Porter (eds) *Aid, NGOs and the Realities of Women's Lives*. Rugby: Practical Action.

Shutt, C. (2009) *Changing the World by Changing Ourselves: Reflections from a Bunch of BINGOs*. Brighton: Institute of Development Studies.

Slim, H. (2021) 'Localization is Self-Determination', *Frontiers in Political Science*, 3, p. 708584. https://doi.org/10.3389/fpos.2021.708584

Sogge, D. (1996) 'Settings and Choices', in D. Sogge (ed.) *Compassion and Calculation: The Business of Private Foreign Aid*. London: Pluto Press.

Sogge, D. and Biekart, K. (1996) 'Calculation, Compassion ... and Choices', in D. Sogge (ed.) *Compassion and Calculation: The Business of Private Foreign Aid*. London: Pluto Press.

Suchman, M. (1995) 'Managing Legitimacy: Strategic and Institutional Approaches', *Academy of Management Review*, 20(3), pp. 571–610. https://doi.org/10.5465/amr.1995.9508080331

Toroma Partnership Project (2011) *Narrative Report to ActionAid May 2011*. Toroma Uganda: TPP.

USAID (2022). *Policy for Localization of Humanitarian Assistance*, Washington, DC: USAID. Available at https://www.humanitarianlibrary.org/sites/default/files/2022/10/DRAFT-USAID-Policy-Localization-of-HA-10242022.pdf

Wallace, T. and Chapman, J. (2004) 'An Investigation into the Reality Behind NGO Rhetoric of Downward Accountability', in L. Earle (ed.) *Creativity and Constraint*. Oxford: INTRAC.

Wallace, T. and Kaplan, A. (2003) *The Taking of the Horizon: Lessons from ActionAid Uganda's Experience of Changes in Development Practice*. ActionAid Impact Assessment Unit Working Paper No. 4. Kampala: ActionAid International.

Wallace, T. and Porter, F. (eds) (2013) *Aid, NGOs and the Realities of Women's Lives: A Perfect Storm*. Rugby: Practical Action.

Wallace, T., Bornstein, L. and Chapman, J. (2007) *The Aid Chain: Coercion and Commitment in Development NGOs*. London: Practical Action.

Walsh, S. and Johnson, O. (2018) *Getting to Zero: A Doctor and a Diplomat on the Ebola Frontline*. London: Zed Books.

Walsh, S.B. (2014) *The Improbability of Accountability of Nongovernmental Organisations to Their Intended Beneficiaries: The Case of ActionAid*. PhD Thesis. London School of Economics and Political Science. Available at: https://etheses.lse.ac.uk/876/

Watkins, S.C., Swidler, A. and Hannan, T. (2012) 'Outsourcing Social Transformation: Development NGOs as Organizations', *Annual Review of Sociology*, 38, pp. 285–315.

Williams, S.A. (2010) 'Intersections of Accountability: Measuring the Effectiveness of International Development NGOs', *Berkeley Journal of Sociology*, 54, pp. 27–58.

World Resources Institute (2022) *Principles for Locally Led Adaptation*. Available at: https://www.wri.org/initiatives/locally-led-adaptation/principles-locally-led-adaptation

Zarnegar Deloffre, M. (2010) 'NGO accountability clubs in the humanitarian sector: social dimensions of club emergence and design', in M.K. Gugerty and P. Aseem (eds) *Voluntary Regulation of NGOs and Nonprofits: An Accountability Club Framework*. Cambridge: Cambridge University Press, pp. 169–200. https://doi.org/10.1017/CBO9780511778933.009

ANNEX 1

Note from Concern setting out their current work and approach to locally led programming

In Concern Worldwide, we believe that local communities affected by crises have the right to lead and shape, via their perspectives and capacities, responses to their own needs. Through our experience working in partnership with national and local actors in some of the world's most fragile and conflict affected countries, we understand that locally led and owned interventions tailored to local environments are more timely, efficient, and effective and that working with partners will create more sustainable and resilient solutions to extreme poverty, humanitarian crises, conflict, and climate change.

We invest in building mutual trust: being accountable to donors to ensure programmes are well-managed; being accountable to partners, and being accountable to the people we serve, to ensure that programmes meet their needs and achieve major improvements in their lives which last and spread without ongoing support from Concern.

Concern's approach identifies five 'pathways' that will strengthen local systems, establish equitable partnerships with local actors, provide quality funding to local actors, strengthen their capacity, and increase the visibility, voice, and agency of local actors and communities – so that the local systems which provide access to goods and services for people affected by crises are meeting local needs.

Concern will continue to invest in locally led programming, with a dedicated team of global and national advisers supporting country programmes to collaborate and share capacity with local/national partners. We are collaborating with other agencies to promote locally led programming; becoming signatories to the 'Charter for Change' and working with fellow members of the Alliance2015 to develop a 'due diligence passporting' approach to simplify the partnership process for local organisations.

ActionAid response, 12th June 2025

ActionAid welcomes critical reflection and analysis of our work. We are committed to playing our role to bring about system change to address poverty and injustice, and we recognise learning and adapting is vital to this journey.

Having started out as a UK based charity in 1972, ActionAid made a move from its 25-year history of needs-based work to lay out a vision of a rights-based approach in its 1998 strategy Fighting Poverty Together. This was a key catalyst also for internal change.

In the early 2000s ActionAid sought to transform its own management and governance structures in line with its politics – through a process known as internationalisation. This led to the creation of a federation with national boards and assemblies in most countries, and a Global Secretariat, headquartered in South Africa. We have recently been documenting this to draw out learning from our processes of shifting power internally.

Our commitment to participatory approaches has been steadfast throughout this period. We use a human rights-based approach, promoting a cycle of reflection and action, to build the agency of people living in poverty, encouraging them to analyse and transform power at a local and national level.

ActionAid's Accountability, Learning and Planning System (ALPS), referenced in the book, was a further attempt to look at our own practice of power, both personally and within the organisation – and the principles and approaches laid out there are now widely embedded across the federation. ALPS was itself revised in 2011, and key elements are now included in organisational handbooks and reference materials on our rights-based approach, as well as in our monitoring, evaluation, and learning frameworks.

The research in this book highlights challenges from some of our past efforts to shift power and build agency from below. Whilst this book is not just about our work, we have been picking up lessons from this research since the fieldwork was conducted over 10 years ago. There are no simple or definitive answers, but we have evolved considerably over the years, and it is worth highlighting:

- ActionAid's understanding of a **human rights-based approach** has become more systematised, evolving alongside internationalisation and we have facilitated widespread reflections and analysis of power within the institution. The third edition of our core resource on Human Rights Based Approaches captures some of this: Action for Global Justice in Practice – AA HRBA. To underpin a refocus on participatory methodologies for shifting power, a new website is being launched this year, offering a one-stop-shop to practitioners: www.reflectionaction.org

- **Accountability mechanisms with community members**, particularly women, are more widely embedded, with more meaningful engagement from excluded groups. Regular participatory reviews, interviews, feedback mechanisms, and surveys provide insight into what is driving change and where further effort is needed. Participatory review and reflection processes remain a core mechanism for continuous learning across ActionAid programmes and happen locally, nationally, and internationally every year. Where we come across the sort of dynamics outlined in the book, we critically challenge them. We remain committed to long–term, rooted engagement with people living in poverty and to deepening our accountability to those we work with.

- We recognise that to be a more **effective partner to movements / grassroots organisations** we need to constantly evolve our planning, reporting, budgeting, and accounting systems, recognising that there are power dynamics embedded in every system, policy, and procedure. Our current strategic implementation plan for 2025–2028 has clear priorities laid out for every function and team nationally and internationally (from finance to Human Resources, from IT to communications) – so everyone is conscious of their active role in helping to shift power.

- We have made a renewed commitment to **decolonisation, anti-racism, and shifting power** in our governance systems, management, and partnerships. In 2023, we completed an internal audit of our progress, challenges, and opportunities in these areas that is now being actioned.

- We have championed women's leadership in humanitarian responses. ActionAid's definition of '**women-led localisation**' highlights that localisation must be a transformative process which puts women and girls at its centre and values the significant role of women's leadership at a local level as part of humanitarian action. It also crucially acknowledges the multiple responsibilities that women face, including unpaid care work, and advocates for supportive and practical solutions to address these barriers.

Finally, we agree with the concerns raised in the book about how short-term funding cycles can contradict the aims of transforming power at community level – which depends on long-term engagement. The projectisation of aid remains a major concern for us – with three-year project funding the norm in institutional funding. ActionAid has historically had a long-term funding base through individual giving – with several hundred thousand supporters across 14 countries. Ideally shorter-term donor funding should come to reinforce and build on our longer-term rooted engagement. We are working to weave projects into longer-term transformative programmes, but we are still learning and remain open to critical challenge.

Endnotes

Chapter 1

1. Popularly known as the 'COP', this refers to the United Nations Framework Convention for Climate Change Conference of the Parties, an annual two-week conference which negotiates measures of climate action and reviews progress.
2. There are a lot of different views on terminology here. The term 'beneficiary' has been commonly used when speaking about NGO accountability. I use 'intended beneficiary' in this book to reflect the fact that NGOs are setting out to provide benefits of some kind to the individuals referred to, but whether these benefits are provided or not is another question.
3. The Grand Bargain has been updated but partnership and participation are still central features. The latest version has two focus areas, the first of which is 'Continued support to localisation, participation of affected communities, and quality funding' (Grand Bargain, 2023a, p. 3).

Chapter 2

4. Nowadays there are extremely prominent international NGOs with roots in the Global South, such as BRAC International. This was not evident when I was working on and studying partnership. Hence the international NGOs I am referring to were originally from the Global North.
5. According to Babalola, Lungwangwa, and Adeyinka (1999, cited in Etim, 2016, p. 273): 'structural adjustment programs were measures introduced in the 1980s in third world countries to reduce internal and external deficits, increase efficiency in the economy, and reduce government expenditure. The measure

also involved selling to private interest, government-owned enterprises and reducing subsidies both on consumption items and to products'.

Chapter 3

6. I also observed monitoring visits and other meetings with or about partners to better understand the practice.
7. Concern Worldwide noted, in reading a draft of this book, that the political affiliation of the NGO leaders to the SPLA would now be a red flag in terms of entering into a partnership.

Chapter 5

8. An exhaustive literature review on this topic is available in my PhD thesis (Walsh, 2014) which is available online.

Chapter 6

9. There were subsequently global reviews called *Taking Stock 2* in 2004 and *Taking Stock 3* in 2010.

Chapter 7

10. Full detail on the methodology I used for this research, including a list of interviewees can be found in my PhD thesis (Walsh, 2014).
11. Gottlieb (2006, pp. 47–48) characterises ethnography as offering 'an unparalleled set of methods for exploring and gaining insight into people's values, beliefs and behaviours. Qualitative methods, of which ethnography is the quintessential exemplar ... have the potential to explore ruptures between individuals' stated opinions and beliefs ... on the one hand, and their actual behaviours, on the other hand, since the latter may not always reflect the former'.
12. All photos were taken with the advance permission of those present. Except where otherwise cited, all photographs included in this book are my own.

Chapter 8

13. To give a sense of scale here, total expenditure of ActionAid Uganda in 2003 was £3,226,000 (ActionAid Uganda, 2005b).

Chapter 9

14. It is commonly said in the literature on downward accountability that upward accountability, such as reporting to donors, is a major barrier and takes time away from participatory processes and other community engagement. This may well be the case in many organisations, but was not my experience in Concern or researching ActionAid. This may relate to their funding structures as both had very significant public funding, balanced with their institutional funding. When I worked on localisation with Concern, my work was entirely funded by unrestricted donations and donor requirements were not at all a barrier to what we were trying to do on partnership and capacity building. With respect to ActionAid Uganda, the funding balance when I was there was 45 per cent from institutional donors and 55 per cent from child sponsorship (ActionAid Uganda, 2012b). While there were no complaints by staff about institutional donors, there were complaints about the workload of sponsorship funding, which I have discussed above.
15. However, one senior staff interviewee was sceptical that ActionAid Uganda staff lacked time and said that the issue was more how they utilised their time: 'This needs to be considered when people talk about workload. We really need to think about performance management. What are people supposed to be doing, are they doing it or are others covering for them'.

Chapter 10

16. This is not necessarily problematic but it's important for donors and NGOs to be aware of political connections of partner leadership so they can understand any relevant power dynamics that might affect the work.
17. Shah (2013) and Lewis (2013) noted another possible motivation for action (or inaction): the desire of staff to enhance their career prospects within an organisation, which is often not helped by 'rocking the boat'.
18. Other literature, such as Mosse (2005), also highlights the hidden power and freedom that even junior staff can have, as long as they maintain the correct representations of the project for colleagues further up the hierarchy.

Chapter 11

19. Interviewees related turnover in ActionAid Uganda to issues such as low recognition of performance, poor career

development opportunities, heavy workload leading to stress, and relatively low salaries – inflation of approximately 30 per cent in Uganda in 2011 was mentioned as playing a role here (ActionAid Uganda, 2012a). On the positive side, many interviewees noted that ActionAid staff members were considered to be well-trained within the sector, which enables them to get better jobs.

20. Anthony Wasswa was Country Director until 1998 and John Bulega was interim Country Director in 2004.

21. There was a lot of talk in my interviews of the perceived 'imposition' of the shifts to partnership and the human rights-based approach, but there are other considerations here which are outside the scope of my study. For instance, it was expressed by a senior staff member that some ActionAid staff prefer to do direct service delivery because it is easier in various ways and provides more job security for ActionAid staff, but that this is not a sustainable approach. Therefore, strong leadership and often simply just new rules and systems were needed to convince staff to work in more sustainable ways, such as through partnership and the human rights-based approach, whether or not this was their preference.

22. David and Mancini (2004, p. 7) list the team that created ALPS as: Ephraim Dhlembeu (the Africa Programme Coordinator), Lubna Ehsan (Pakistan Gender Policy Analyst), Colin Williams (Africa Director), Nigel Saxby-Soffe (Director of Finance), Robert Chambers (Trustee), and Rosalind David (Head of Impact Assessment Unit).

23. Interestingly the management response's five references to how a 'revised version of ALPS' would contribute to solving other issues did not relate to the issues in the ALPS review but other issues around partnership, leadership, programme quality, planning, and learning (ActionAid, 2004). This illustrated significant faith in what a set of guidelines can do.

Chapter 12

24. There was an argument made to me that productivity and efficiency were real issues in ActionAid and that excess workload was not always a valid complaint. This may well be true, but judging that was beyond the scope of my research. What is important here is that their perception of excess workload caused stress for staff.

25. 'Eating money' is a common expression in Uganda for people diverting official money for personal use.

26. Many fraud cases were brought to light by ActionAid's active internal audit unit. This unit maintained an 'audit query matrix' which, for instance, contained the 613 audit queries mentioned for 2011, the vast majority relating to partners, of which 304 were resolved during the year (ActionAid Uganda, 2011). These queries may be due to weak capacity rather than fraud. Whistle-blowing is another mechanism which exposed fraud and led, for instance, to five cases being investigated in 2008 (ActionAid Uganda, 2009b).

Chapter 13

27. New public management is closely associated with managerialism: both have neoliberal roots and are focused on bringing private-sector methodologies into public administration (Goetz and Jenkins, 2002).
28. Newman (2011, p. 222), on the other hand, found that ActionAid had largely rejected the management discourse with its neoliberal assumptions. One point of note in this discussion, as Newman pointed out, was that, unlike some of its peers in the UK, ActionAid had not yet recruited a chief executive from the private sector.
29. While there is room for service delivery within ActionAid's human rights-based approach, this is limited. This tension between the human rights-based approach and participation of communities in ActionAid is the core finding of the study by Newman (2011).

Chapter 14

30. Aristotle defined rhetoric as 'an ability, in each [particular] case, to see the available means of persuasion' (Aristotle, 1991, p. 1355; Sellars, 2006, p. 59). While often seen in modern journalism as inherently misleading, in academic writing this is not necessarily the case, the common feature of rhetoric being that it is intended to influence the audience (Kennedy, 2001).
31. Optics is defined as 'the aspects of an action, policy, or decision (as in politics or business) that relate to public perceptions' (Merriam-Webster, 2024).
32. One definition by the European Commission (no date) is as follows: 'A Logical Framework is a matrix in which the intervention logic (overall objective, purpose, expected results and activities), assumptions, objectively verifiable indicators and

sources of verification are presented. It is used as a management tool to *improve the design of Interventions*. It involves identifying strategic elements (inputs, outputs, outcomes, impact) and their relationships, indicators, and the assumptions or risks that may influence the success or failure of a Project'.

33. I am using American Sociologist Mark Suchman's (1995, p. 574) definition of legitimacy here, of legitimacy as 'a generalized perception that the actions of an entity are desirable, proper, or appropriate within some socially constructed system of norms, values, beliefs, and definitions'. This definition echoes many others in the literature, particularly in its focus of legitimacy as a shifting concept that depends on perceptions of particular stakeholders or groups of stakeholders at particular times (cf. Brown and Jagadananda, 2007, p. 7).

34. Official development assistance, commonly known as aid.

Index

Pakistan, 11, 24, 27, 28, 29, 34,
87, 162
Pallisa, 52, 75, 76, 78, 105
Participant observation, 53
Participatory review and
reflection processes, 156
Philippines, 95, 121, 124
political correctness, 5, 18, 32,
34, 136

resource dependency theory,
110, 122
results-based management, 108,
109, 110, 120, 121
Rosalind David, 106, 162
Rwanda, 11, 21, 24

Scott-Smith, 115, 123, 151
Scott-Smith, T. *See* Scott-Smith
Scott-Villiers, 45, 46, 89, 98, 151
Scott-Villiers, Patta.
See Scott-Villiers
Seibel, 126, 151
Seibel, W. *See* Seibel
Shetty, 44, 45, 46, 71

Shetty, Salil. *See* Shetty
social audit, 55, 79
Sogge, 84, 92, 138, 151
Sogge, David. *See* Sogge
South Sudan, 11, 12, 14, 24,
25, 26, 27, 28, 29, 30,
31, 32, 34, 37, 61, 101,
126, 136
Staff turnover, 6, 84

Tanzania, 121, 122
Transparency boards, 6, 116, 119
Trend-jumping, 6, 83, 84

USAID, 9, 15, 16, 17, 152

Vadera, 59, 60, 96
Vadera, Meenu. *See* Vadera

Wallace, 45, 84, 85, 96, 107,
109, 110, 120, 121, 147,
149, 150, 151, 152
Wallace, Tina. *See* Wallace
Weisband, 77, 145, 148, 149
Weisband, E. *See* Weisband

www.ingramcontent.com/pod-product-compliance
Lightning Source LLC
Chambersburg PA
CBHW051258020426
42333CB00026B/3256